ONE SUMMER DAY IN AMERICA

July 13, 1954

JIM MOLLENKOPF

Lake of the Cat Publishing
P.O. Box 351454
Toledo, OH 43635-1454
www.lakeofthecat.com

CONTENTS

DEDICATION

To Clevelanders everywhere

FOREWORD

It was a hot summer day in America and life was good. The prosperity that followed World War II was in full flourish—the baby boom generation filled maternity wards, new homes were built as suburbs exploded past city limits, and jobs were plentiful. The generation now in place whose parents had suffered through the Great Depression was clearly going to live better than their folks, and in many cases, much better; on this very day, the Commerce Department announced that the nation's production had set a new record for the fourth consecutive year. The American Dream was being dreamed like never before and the reach of the national horizon seemed to be infinite.

In sports, baseball reigned supreme as the National Pastime and in the giant ballpark in Cleveland, Ohio, on this day, the game's royalty gathered for the annual Midsummer Classic, the All Star game. A sweltering crowd filled the stadium on the Lake Erie shore that day and the wealth of talent on the field reflected the affluence off of it.

Few in the crowd likely realized that nearly one-third of the players and both managers would someday be enshrined in one of the most exclusive clubs in the world, the Baseball Hall of Fame. It was the Golden Age of Baseball and men whose names are now carved in the Rosetta stone of baseball legend such as Mickey Mantle, Jackie Robinson, Ted Williams, Willie Mays, Stan Musial, Yogi Berra, Whitey Ford, and Casey Stengel walked the field of green. And when the contest was over, records had fallen and they had played the most exciting game in All Star history, before or since.

Among those players were men whose presence would have been impossible as few as 7 years earlier, as 5 black All Stars—4 of African-American descent—were on the field. It was not until 1947 when Jackie Robinson and owner Branch Rickey of the Brooklyn Dodgers, followed by Larry Doby and owner Bill Veeck of the Cleveland Indians broke the six-decade color barriers in the National and American leagues, respectively. Both Robinson and Doby were on the field this day, trailblazers who had run the gauntlet of white venom and fear to get this far and paved the way for others. By 1954, the abuse they'd endured was dying down and black children playing little league baseball all over the country could seriously dream of playing in the big leagues some day.

The social change taking place in baseball was reflected less so in society as a whole. America largely remained divided along separate and unequal racial lines, the postwar prosperity and better paying jobs primarily benefitting white America—the new suburbs for whites only. In fact it had only been a couple of months earlier that the "separate but equal" doctrine as applied to schools was ruled to be inherently unequal by the Supreme Court. But the change taking place in baseball helped pave the way to a larger societal change, something Jackie Robinson and Larry Doby probably little realized the day they took their first nervous steps on a major league baseball field 7 years earlier.

America was at peace that summer day in 1954. The Korean War had ended a year earlier, but it was an uneasy peace, cast against the atomic backdrop of the Cold War. Earlier in the year, Secretary of State John Foster Dulles announced a policy of massive retaliation in the event of an attack by the-then Soviet Union against the United States, two countries deeply suspicious of each other.

In otherwise heady times, the haunting apparition of an enormous mushroom cloud loomed both over the American landscape and in the American psyche. Some of the basements in downtown Cleveland buildings, as in other American cities and towns, were being designated as fallout shelters, marked by ominous black and yellow signs, where people could go to escape the radioactive particles that would rain from the sky after a nuclear blast.

This book is a snapshot of that summer day at the game, and the players and other events, major and mundane, both in Cleveland and in the United States of America, using newspapers as the source. Nineteen fifty-four was part of a decade that in following years has been idealized as a simpler time, one of black and white innocence, social consensus, and general lack of discord. This effort is not an attempt to draw any broad conclusions or place that day or decade in any theoretical context.

The daily newspaper was still the king of the media world at that time and a staple of American life. They were as common in the living room as a lamp or a chair. Cleveland still had three dailies while New York City had seven. Nationally, more than 1,700 daily papers landed on doorsteps or were hawked by newsboys as the curious, new and visual, electronic medium of television was still in its relative infancy. The newspaper in 1954 was still, without doubt, the number one source of news and information.

When the decade began, less than 10 percent of American homes could receive a TV signal, a number that grew to more than 85 percent by decade's end. Of course that innocent-seeming newborn—there were about 5 million TV sets sold per year in the 1950s—would eventually lead to a revolution in electronic media, knocking the newspaper from its throne. And as the second decade of the twenty-first century begins, the sun seems to be setting, sadly, on the American newspaper.

PROLOGUE

On a July day in 1796, along the quiet and heavily forested Lake Erie shore came a party of 50 led by a surveyor named Moses Cleaveland, a Yale-educated, Connecticut Yankee hired by the Connecticut Land Company to survey the 3 million acres of wilderness called Western Reserve. On the 22nd day, they landed at the mouth of the Cuyahoga River and from this, the city of Cleveland, as it was later shortened to, was born. Moses returned east by summer's end and died 10 years later—never to see the city that bore his name.

The federal census taker who passed through in April 1800, had an easy job as Cleveland had but a single resident, one Lorenzo Carter. As the year went on, the population shot up to seven. Those first residents struggled, plagued by disease and all the other issues that come with trying to make a life in a frontier wilderness—well beyond the edge of what was then civilization.

The next 10 years weren't much better as a stagnant channel of the Cuyahoga continued to produce disease-carrying mosquitoes that dampened the new hamlet's appeal. The settlers knew they were getting sick but had no idea why. And there was Mr. Carter, not exactly a one-man Chamber of Commerce. He discouraged new settlers who came through, telling them the sand-clogged harbor would never be opened and there was no money to be made, meanwhile cornering the market on Indian trade for himself to the tune of about $1,000 annually. He had also organized a loose group of backwoods itinerants and drunks to do his bidding, paying them with board and whiskey. When the War of 1812 broke out, Cleveland was a small and struggling outpost.

By 1824, however, things were moving for the city, with nine stores, three taverns, a newspaper, and six sailing vessels plying Lake Erie for trade. The following year, the opening of the Erie Canal provided a transportation and trade route all way to New York City, and when Cleveland was selected to be the northern terminus for the Ohio and Erie Canal connecting Lake Erie and the Ohio River, growth was assured. When the Civil War broke out in 1861, Cleveland was a small but handsome, city of about 44,000 residents, primarily commercial in business affairs and Eastern in personality.

But between the demand for weapons and other materials for that war, followed by the Industrial Revolution of the 1870s, the city literally exploded into a manufacturing and industrial center. Much of that production was located in the Flats, an urban canyon along downtown Cleveland's edge, carved by the serpentine course of the Cuyahoga River over the millennia, the eastern and western plateaus nearly a mile apart in places.

A Civil War captain named Willard Glazier, who traveled the country extensively in the years after the war, stood on the high west side of the Flats in 1880. Where cattle had pastured not too many years earlier, "the view, though far from beautiful, is a very interesting one. There are copper smelting, iron rolling, and iron manufacturing works, lumber yards, paper mills, breweries, flour mills, nail works, pork-packing establishments and the multitudinous industries of a great manufacturing city … the scene at night, from this same elevated position, is picturesque in the extreme. The whole valley shows a black background lit up with a thousand points of light from factories, foundries, and steamboats which are multiplied into two thousand as they are reflected in the waters of the Cuyahoga which looks like a silver ribbon flowing through the blackness."

The city's industrial transformation led to a human one as labor was needed, lots of it, and lots of it now. Cleveland opened its doors to the world and through those doors, the world walked. From every corner of Europe and beyond, immigrants flocked to the city in the years after the Civil War and into the new century to work in the steel mills or hammer that steel into finished products. By the 1920s, the city was a colorful human tapestry of nearly 50 nationalities with more foreign language newspapers than anywhere in the country.

They were German, Irish, English, and Italian. They were also Hungarian, Serbian, Greek, and Russian Jews. A Czech immigrant, landing in 1889, later wrote that he was amazed and pleased to find a neighborhood where his native tongue was spoken for blocks around. He was substantially less than pleased at his first glimpse of the Cuyahoga River, which had been transformed into an urban and industrial sewer, in sad contrast to the rivers of home. A fellow Czech tried to put it into perspective telling him, "My boy, you must forget Bohemia; you're in America now."

From America they came too, the rural South in particular, poor blacks and whites leaving behind back-breaking work on the farm and streaming north for back-breaking work in the factories, but for a lot more pay. In what's been called The Great Migration, Cleveland's African-American population grew by 300 percent in the 1920s.

That decade in particular was one of tremendous growth downtown, capped off by the construction of Terminal Tower, an elegant spire reaching more than 700 feet in the air and the tallest office building outside New York City when it first cast its shadow over the statues and monuments of Public Square. Clevelanders gazed up at it with pride while under their feet, dozens of trains a day rumbled into Union Terminal buried underground deep beneath the tower.

Rocked badly by the Great Depression in the 1930s, Cleveland recovered during the World War II years. A writer for *The New York Times Magazine*, L. H. Robbins, visited the city in 1946 during the city's 150th birthday celebration and noted, "Clevelanders display an exuberant enthusiasm for their town and their way of life as you don't recall ever noting in any city east of the Alleghenies." He went on to observe how good-natured the downtown crowds were and how they told him how much they liked their city and wouldn't live anywhere else.

In addition to its heart and spirit, the writer Robbins was similarly impressed with Cleveland's bricks and mortar. "From the [Public]

Square, fine avenues spread like ribs of a fan, and their banks, hotels, department stores and office buildings carry on the good work of making the visitor gape. At hand, moreover, toward the lakeshore, are the public buildings; among them the stately library, the auditorium, and a stadium in which an ordinary eastern ballpark would rattle around. Here is a civic center to shout about."

Robbins was also impressed by Cleveland's "huge bridges" although he was far from the first to be. In 1905, an astonished visitor scrawled on a postcard, "There are the greatest lot of bridges here you ever saw." And that was before the advent of the automobile led to the building of the most spectacular ones, including the Hope Memorial Bridge finished in 1932. Eight, massive, Art Deco, sandstone figures, the "Guardians of Traffic," stand silent sentry at both east and west entrances, four at each end. They look more like they belong rising from the sands of Egypt than from the top of a bridge in Ohio.

Originally called the Lorain-Carnegie, this bridge was renamed in the 1980s for the family of the late comedian Bob Hope who spent his childhood in Cleveland. Hope and his family were a part of Cleveland's immigrant tapestry, his father William bringing them there from England in 1908. The skilled, stonemason hands of William Hope are believed to have helped shape the impressive figures on the bridge that now bears the family name.

As the year 1954 dawned, Cleveland remained a brawny, smoking, industrial powerhouse, the country's seventh largest city with upward of a million residents. There were cracks in the urban infrastructure to be sure, fissures that would widen in later years. But not this year. Not this day. Cleveland was still a civic center to shout about, as L. H. Robbins asserted, and the city itself was ready to shout on July 13. For the sporting event second only in importance to the World Series had the city on the national stage.

PREGAME

A midsummer heatwave gripped the Midwest, the thermometer topping out at 94 the day before. The sun cracked the hazy eastern horizon at 6:05 A.M. and slowly lit the land as Clevelanders woke from a fitful, perspiring sleep, the hum of room fans filling their ears in the days when home air conditioning was still a novelty. It was Tuesday, but not an ordinary one as tens of thousands headed downtown, not to their jobs but to Municipal Stadium on Lake Erie's shore.

They came from the east along the Memorial Shoreway, an eight-lane concrete ribbon hugging the lakeshore that predated the interstate highway system. From the west, they crossed over the Flats on Cleveland's famed bridges into downtown. From the air, they landed at Lakefront Airport, which was the busiest it had been in years with more than 200 light aircraft arriving. And they poured out of Cleveland's sold-out downtown hotels, including the Hotel Hollenden, where more than 400 sportswriters from both North and South America were headquartered.

To cavernous Municipal Stadium they came—a two-deck affair completed in 1931 that at the time boasted the largest seating capacity of any outdoor arena in the world—a stadium so big that no home-run ball would *ever* reach its center-field bleachers. With a listed capacity of more than 78,000, the wide concourse of its lower deck could accommodate thousands more. In 1948, an astonishing 86,000 people jammed in to see a World Series game between the Cleveland Indians and the Boston Braves, some climbing and sitting on steel girders and others packing in behind the outfield fence. There would be no need to stand or sit on girders this day as the crowd of nearly 69,000 would be handily accommodated. It was the second largest crowd in All Star game history, surpassed only by the 1935 gathering in the same stadium.

The sun rose into a blistering blue sky as thousands waited for the gates to open. Last-minute bargains waited at the ticket windows where a standing room ticket could be had for $2 and a bleacher seat for only a buck.

Once inside, they climbed to their seats in the high concrete stands and trained their binoculars on National League All Stars such as Jackie Robinson, Stan Musial, Duke Snider, and Willie Mays, as they took batting practice—players they'd never seen in person before as there was no interleague play then. Fans took in the star-studded field before them, bought cold drinks and souvenirs, fanned themselves with programs and rubbed sun lotion on their faces. Kids reached over the railings near the dugouts with paper and pencil, hoping for an All Star autograph—so many star players so close.

A throng of sportswriters headed for the stadium as well. Their idol, the Dean of American Sportswriters, Grantland Rice, was not among them. It was he who in 1924 dubbed the Notre Dame backfield the Four Horseman, from the biblical reference, the four horsemen of the Apocalypse.

Outlined against a blue-gray October sky the Four Horsemen rode again. In dramatic lore they are known as famine, pestilence, destruction and death. These are only aliases. Their real names are: Stuhldreher, Miller, Crowley and Layden. They formed the crest of the South Bend cyclone before which another fighting Army team was swept over the precipice at the Polo Grounds this afternoon as 55,000 spectators peered down upon the bewildering panorama spread out upon the green plain below.

As the writers packed the press boxes, Rice was in a Manhattan office, turning in his syndicated column, which happened to be on Willie Mays, who, in his first year back from the Army, was taking the baseball world by storm. Rice wanted to get a little more work done before watching the All Star game on television that afternoon. He was 73, now, and hadn't been feeling well lately, writing to a friend about a week earlier, "listening to your arteries harden isn't such bad sport after all." Suddenly he fell to the floor, gravely ill.

He would never hear the crack of a bat again as he was pronounced dead of a stroke at New York's Roosevelt Hospital in the early evening. His honorary pallbearers at his overflow funeral later that week included the legendary golfer Bobby Jones and boxers Jack Dempsey and Gene Tunney. Later that year, the Football Writers Association of America named the trophy it gives to the college football team—the group it judges to be the best in America—the Grantland Rice Trophy, a name in use today.

Around 1:15 P.M., it was time for the usual, pre-game meeting at home plate between the umpires and team managers to go over any ground rules, and exchange line-up cards and light hearted banter. At the helm for the American League was New York Yankee Manager Charles Dillon (Casey) Stengel while the skipper for the National League was Walter Alston of the Brooklyn Dodgers. Both managers were destined for the Hall of Fame. Any other similarity on this day ended right there.

Walter Alston was a 7-year-old cherub growing up in small town Ohio in 1919 when Casey Stengel grabbed his bat in old Ebbets Field, playing for the Pittsburgh Pirates against his former team, the Brooklyn Dodgers. Booing and taunting were high art forms among baseball fans in those days, and the serious practitioners of the craft were really bestowing it on Casey, who had a slight smile tugging on the corners of his mouth as he approached home plate. Earlier in the dugout, he somehow had gotten his hands on a sparrow that he carefully tucked under his cap. He reached the plate as the artful abuse poured down from above, turned and faced the crowd, and paused for a second. He then bowed and tipped his cap and the startled bird fluttered up in the air and away as the stadium roared with laughter. A legend was born.

After a solid career as a major league player—his early aspirations of being a dentist went by the wayside—Stengel was in his 15th year as a manager and sixth with the Yankees where his record was merely perfect. He could have decorated all the fingers on one hand with World Series rings as the Yankees had won five consecutive titles under his guidance, going 20–8 in those Series games against the best teams the National League could throw at them.

Alston, on the other hand, was a virtual unknown—an article in the *Cleveland Plain Dealer Sunday Magazine* a couple of days earlier carried the headline, "Who is Walter Alston?" In his first season as a major league manager—Alston would literally be seeing his first All Star game ever—the career minor league player had been plucked from obscurity by the Dodgers. He had been managing out of the country the previous 4 years, running the club's top farm team—the Montreal Royals.

Brooklyn's previous manager, Charlie Dressen, had been let go despite winning the 1952 and 1953 National League pennants. His crime was asking for a multiyear contract, a Dodger taboo, and Dressen's door closing was Walter Alston's opening. He walked through that door and did not walk back out for 23 years, managing the Dodgers until 1976, and in the process, signing 23 one-year contracts.

Alston was a graduate of the University of Miami in Ohio, at a time when college graduates were rare in baseball. Alston was studious, laid back, and business-like. Stengel, on the other hand, was a character and a clown and one for whom the phrase "holding court" could have been invented. Nicknamed "The Old Perfesser," the locker room was his lecture hall and the media his attentive students who gathered round for his pre- and postgame monologues on all things baseball and variety of other subjects too. He frequently punctuated his impromptu lectures with his trademark assertion, "You could look it up."

He once responded to a reporter's question with a 40-minute ramble when the frustrated scribe finally said, "Casey, you haven't answered my question." Stengel looked at the man with a touch of surprise and said, "Don't rush me." Although the volume of words tumbling from him might have been great, the clarity was somewhat less so than that. The way he turned a phrase, his odd choice of words and his unique slant on things in general became known as "Stengelese," a vernacular that could be interpreted by the hometown reporters, but left its share of out-of-town writers scratching their heads. The day before the game, he expounded on the challenges of selecting players in general. "It's hard to choose and you can take that catch which Snider made in Philadelphia and which they say was the greatest ever but Mays makes eight better since then and just the other day in Washington I never saw a better one in my life the way that feller grabs the ball and what did Mays do in the 1951 World Series? Like I say, it's hard to decide." And in 1958 he delivered 45 minutes of generally baffling testimony before a U.S. Senate committee during a baseball antitrust hearing, saying among other things, "I had many years that I was not so successful as a ballplayer, as it is a game of skill."

Whether it was mugging for a photographer or directing his teams to 10 pennants and 6 World Series titles, Casey Stengel deeply loved, and thoroughly knew, the game of baseball. He would manage a total of 25 seasons before retiring from the New York Mets in 1965. And his American League team was counting on his knowledge this day as it had lost four straight years to the National League, a fact of which Casey was painfully aware as he had managed the American League squad in all four of those losses. The meeting at home plate broke up, the managers headed back to their dugouts, and the umpires trotted to their positions in the field.

As the fans in the stands waited for the start of the game, conversation was not about baseball, but about Cleveland's "crime of the century." Less than week-and-a-half earlier in the darkness of the early morning of July 4, pretty, pregnant, Marilyn Sheppard slept in her bed in the suburban Bay Village home on the Lake Erie shore she shared with her husband, Dr. Sam Sheppard, a young osteopath. Some time before dawn, an attacker with a blunt object loomed over her and rained blow after blow, more than two dozen in all, about her head and face. Blood spattered the walls as she breathed her last.

Her husband Sam claimed he was sleeping downstairs when he heard her scream and ran to her room to find a "bushy haired man" standing over her. This man then struck Sam in the head, knocking him unconscious. He awoke minutes later, ran downstairs, and chased the man out of the house and down to the beach where he tackled him before he was struck and knocked unconscious again. He awoke with the waves of Lake Erie lapping around him, returned to the house in a daze and checked on his wife who was obviously beyond help. He then called his neighbor who was also the Bay Village mayor and reported what had happened.

Although Marilyn Sheppard was dead, the story of her tragic demise was as alive as could be. The event was a major story in newspapers across the country and even in Europe. But locally, it exploded in the Cleveland papers like no crime story had before. It had all the ingredients of sensational crime drama: A handsome, young doctor and talented surgeon with a beautiful wife, murdered in her own bed in the dark of the night at the hands of a mysterious stranger in an idyllic, affluent, suburb where such things don't happen.

As many Cleveland-area residents became increasingly fascinated with the crime, a steady stream of cars began driving by the crime scene, snapping photographs of the Sheppard home and some persons even walking into the yard and peering into the house through the windows. In the few days immediately after the murder, the public had been sympathetic toward Sheppard who had been hospitalized with head and neck injuries ostensibly inflicted by the intruder. But as the investigation continued—the case was handed over to the Cleveland Police Department—another, less than idyllic picture of Sam Sheppard's world began to emerge—that of self-centered, womanizer who'd had affairs over the years and whose marriage was in trouble—the focus became increasingly on him.

Police investigating the murder were finding his version of events to be incredulous and the three daily Cleveland newspapers were becoming increasingly sensational and hostile in their coverage, the circulation-hungry *Cleveland Press* in particular, whose treatment of the story became tabloid-like in character and intensity. Every day for the rest of July, Sundays excepted when the *Press* did not publish, the paper ran page one, top headline coverage of the murder including editorials and cartoons attacking not only Sheppard but investigators for not doing what was obvious to the *Press*—charge him with the crime.

On July 20, the paper ran a page one editorial with the headline, "Somebody Is Getting Away With Murder." On July 30, the paper ramped up the pressure with another page one editorial with the headline, "Why Isn't Sam Sheppard in Jail?" which in the day's later editions was changed to, "Quit Stalling and Bring Him In!" That evening, Sam Sheppard was arrested and eventually charged with first degree murder, despite the admission of the Cleveland police chief a few days earlier that, even though he personally felt Sam was guilty, there was not "a single shred of evidence against him."

The *Press* was ruled by longtime and legendary editor, Louis B. Seltzer. Dapper in dress and diminutive in stature, his shadow loomed large over the newspaper, one that reached across the country. In fact the July 10, 1954, issue of *The Saturday Evening Post* on the newsstands featured a lengthy article on him titled, "The Noisy Newsboy of Cleveland."

He cared deeply about the city of Cleveland and about the quality of his paper and drove his reporters toward that end. He also preferred a loose, relaxed newsroom where practical jokes were standard practice. On one occasion, a reporter's phone conversation with a Cleveland society woman was interrupted by a loud explosion. When she demanded to know what the noise was, the reporter sheepishly informed her that a lit firecracker had been tossed under his chair. When the indignant woman made it clear that "Mr. Seltzer" would hear about it, the reporter was forced to admit, "Maam, he's the one who threw it."

He was tireless when it came rooting out corruption and misbehavior in the public arena and though he rarely wrote editorials, he personally wrote the Sam Sheppard ones lest someone else take the heat. He sincerely believed Sheppard probably killed his wife and was getting special treatment because he was a doctor and because the Bay Village community had thrown up a protective wall around him. In a later autobiography, Seltzer said he would do the same thing again.

The trial began the following October, with around 60 reporters covering the case, about half of them from out of town. Many of the out-of-town scribes were amazed at the hold the murder had on so many in the Cleveland area. The summer and early fall had been one of rumor, innuendo, and gossip galore about the personal and sex lives of both Sam and Marilyn Sheppard (Marilyn allegedly had an affair with the Bay Village mayor Sam first reported the crime to), their circle of neighbors and friends, and the Bay Village community itself, which had been portrayed in both the local and national media as some sort of elitist, hedonistic playground where people did such things as jump from bed to bed and murder their wives and expect to get away with it. As a result, a sort of class resentment had developed locally: Who do those people living out there think they are?

In addition, it was easier for people to believe that Sam had done it, rather than an intruder. For if a stranger could enter the Sheppard's home in the dark of the night and brutally shatter their American Dream lives and get away with it, then it could happen to anyone.

The trial lasted about 2 months and, despite the lack of evidence connecting Sam directly to Marilyn's murder, he never stood a chance. The trial was presided over by a judge who, in a private conversation that was revealed years later, expressed his belief in Sam's guilt before the proceeding even started and allowed hearsay evidence during it. The trial was also held in a community that fully expected a conviction, a sentiment the jurors were keenly aware of, and with a powerful newspaper establishment that promised political fallout for those police officials and prosecutors who failed to bring one about.

Just before Christmas, Sam Sheppard was convicted of second-degree murder and sentenced to life in prison with eligibility for parole after 10 years. The out-of-town reporters, as a whole, were stunned by the verdict. Sam Sheppard may very well have killed his wife but the prosecution had not proved it, or even come close, went the general consensus. Star columnist for Hearst Newspapers, Dorothy Kilgallen wrote, "It is the first time I have ever been scared by the jury system, and I mean scared."

Christmas came and Cleveland a breathed a sigh of relief that the case was finally over, or so it seemed. Sam Sheppard continued to maintain his innocence and carried on his fight from behind prison walls, filing several appeals, finally achieving success 10 years later when a federal district court judge ordered the State of Ohio to release him or grant a new trial. The U.S. Supreme Court agreed, noting Sheppard had been denied due process due to the "carnival atmosphere," among other errors that surrounded his original trial.

He was released and retried in 1966 with a rising, young criminal defense attorney named F. Lee Bailey as his counsel. He was found not guilty this time although it turned out to be a Pyrrhic victory as he would live less than four more years. He was now drinking heavily and, after a failed attempt to return to medicine, briefly toured as a professional wrestler, capitalizing on his infamy and going by the moniker "The Killer." He died of liver failure in April 1970, at the age of 46. When Sam Sheppard was lowered into the ground in a Columbus cemetery his story, again, was finally over, or so it seemed.

But his son, Sam Reese Sheppard, a 7-year-old sleeping in an adjacent bedroom when his mother was murdered, never accepted that his father killed his mother and campaigned to clear his Dad's name. He filed a wrongful imprisonment suit against the state of Ohio and in the late 1990s both his parents' bodies were exhumed for DNA testing. In 1999, the PBS series *Nova* ran an episode titled, "On the Trail of a Killer," which presented some compelling new evidence gathered by the younger Sheppard and his legal team pointing the finger of guilt away from his father and toward a window washer named Richard Eberling. He had done work in the Sheppard home around the time of the murder, had been convicted of murdering a woman in 1983 and quite possibly had murdered another woman in 1962. And, according to a fellow inmate, had admitted, even bragged that he murdered Marilyn Sheppard before he died in prison in 1998.

In 2000, the civil trial began against the state of Ohio in which dozens of witnesses were called and hundreds of exhibits considered.

During the proceeding, Sam Sheppard the elder was essentially tried by the state's defense for the third time for his wife's murder even though he'd been dead for more than 30 years, the reasoning being that there was no wrongful imprisonment if he actually did it. After a 10-week trial, the jury held unanimously that Sam Reese Sheppard had failed to prove his case.

So Sam Sheppard's story finally did come to an end, except in the minds of older Cleveland area residents who still talk about it. In the end, somebody did get away with murder. After his exhumation, Sam's remains were cremated and interred in a suburban Cleveland cemetery mausoleum with Marilyn's coffin, together again after being separated by a killing on warm July night on the shore of Lake Erie in 1954.

As the crowd and the sportswriters settled in at the stadium, so did the television people, specifically the crew from NBC with play-by-play announcer Mel Allen, the popular voice of the Yankees. Melvin Allen Israel was a young student just finishing up law school at the University of Alabama in 1936, where he broadcast Crimson Tide football games, when he loaded his father's car with some buddies and drove 36 straight hours for a Christmas break vacation in New York City. He gawked at the buildings in Manhattan as he made his way to the CBS studios on Fifth Avenue and presented a card from his Alabama radio station that entitled him to a tour. The manager who greeted him, and who had heard of his football work, asked if he was there for the audition. "What audition?" Mel asked. The rest is broadcasting history as Mel Allen would never practice law and Alabama would never get its native son back.

Radio ruled the airwaves in the days before television and the newly hired, youthful Allen was a small fish in a big pond. But he impressed his bosses the following summer when he was assigned to broadcast the Vanderbilt Cup auto race from an airplane over nearby Long Island—the plane was needed to scoop NBC which had exclusive rights to ground coverage of the event, such was radio competition in those days.

The race was delayed nearly an hour by rain before Mel signed off and the plane returned to the airport. But he had filled that entire period with entertaining, ad lib conversation—no fluke because he believed in thorough preparation for any assignment, something the CBS brass noticed.

On his days off, Allen took the subway to Yankee Stadium, sat high in the stands, and broadcast the game quietly to himself. He dreamed of broadcasting games there someday, something that would have been impossible then as the three New York teams had an agreement to keep games off the air, fearing that broadcasts would hurt attendance. Only Opening Day and World Series games went out over the airwaves.

Allen did broadcast the 1938 Series, a four-game Yankee sweep and his first crack at doing baseball, and the antiradio pact was not renewed after that year. In 1939, the Yankees and Giants partnered for broadcasts of home games, as one team would be at home while the other was on the road, and Allen tried for and was edged out for one of the two jobs. He was about to walk away from broadcasting and go home to Alabama to practice law when luck, and an announcer's lousy judgment, intervened.

About 6 weeks into the season, one of the Giants-Yankees announcers mispronounced Ivory Soap as "Ovary" Soap during a spot, doing it two more times and finding the whole thing to be hilarious. Considerably less amused was soap sponsor Proctor & Gamble who demanded his head. Mel got his job, despite being only 26 years old and having a baseball broadcasting resume of exactly four games. He was careful to pronounce Ivory, and the name every other sponsor's products correctly, and work product names into the play-by-play, something sponsors absolutely loved.

Later his first season, Allen was in the Yankee Stadium broadcast booth for one of the most touching moments in sports history. July 4, 1939, was set aside to honor beloved Yankee great Lou Gehrig, who had been diagnosed with the fatal disease amyotrophic lateral sclerosis just a few weeks earlier, a disease since named for him. Gehrig told the crowd, "Today, I consider myself the luckiest man on the face of the earth," while tears dripped off the cheeks of players and fans alike.

About a year later, Gehrig was brought to the Yankee dugout to visit with his former teammates—the man once known as "The Iron Horse" gaunt and clearly ebbing. As his old friends greeted him and ran on the field to practice, Allen found himself sitting alone next to him, not knowing quite what to say to this doomed legend. Gehrig looked at him, patted him on the knee, and told him how much he enjoyed his Yankee game radio broadcasts, and how they were about the only thing keeping him going. Mel thanked him, quickly excused himself, and went down to the dugout tunnel and wept.

World War II came, which sapped the quality of major league baseball as hundreds of players, including many of the game's stars, went off to war. Some teams were fielding players who could not pass their military physicals and interest in the game waned: longtime, New York sportswriter Frank Graham joked that the 1945 World Series between the Cubs and Tigers was, "the fat men versus the tall men at the office picnic."

The Yankees and Giants dropped radio broadcasts in 1943 and that same year, Allen was drafted into the Army and broadcast programs to troops around the world over Armed Forces Radio. He began his shows the way he did the baseball games with his folksy, trademark, "Hello there everybody" which comforted many a homesick GI.

He was discharged in 1946 and resumed his place behind the Yankees' microphone. The war was over, the country was healing, and baseball was king again as fans came back to the ballparks. As the voice of the Yankees, Allen was now a celebrity both in the sports world and in the world of New York society. The Yankees would thoroughly dominate major league baseball in the postwar years, and the senior announcer from the participating teams did the national World Series radio, and later television broadcasts. Allen's voice resonated not only in New York but in millions of American homes through the 1950s and into the 1960s. Across America, his was the very voice of the World Series.

First Inning

The stadium clock ticked toward 1:30 P.M., the Cleveland Summer Orchestra, under a tent in front of the center-field bleachers, played the National Anthem, and the standing throng let out a roar as the last strains echoed off the high roof of the upper deck. After months of anticipation, it was finally time to play ball and Mel Allen's "Hello there everybody," greeted the NBC television audience.

Trotting to the mound for the American League was Yankee pitcher Whitey Ford, appearing in his first of what would be eight All Star games. Ford had made a most auspicious debut in 1950, being brought up from the minors in July and going 9–0 before suffering his first loss. Duty called the next 2 years as Whitey served in the Army during the Korean War, returning in 1953. It was now a year later and he was on his way to being one of the dominant pitchers baseball had ever seen.

Edward Charles Ford was born and raised in Queens, only a few miles by way of the Triborough Bridge from Yankee Stadium. He didn't start pitching until his senior year in high school and the Yankees discovered him after he graduated in 1946 playing sandlot baseball. It was in the minors that his intensely blond hair earned him the nickname Whitey. Although he may not have had an overpowering fastball or an explosive curve, he had the control of a brain surgeon and was not above a little chicanery; a little dirt rubbed on a ball obscures part of it as it rotates toward home plate, making it hard to pick up.

One umpire said that there was not a "human being on earth who could dirty a ball like Whitey Ford." And well after his Hall of Fame career was over, he finally admitted he sometimes rubbed a little home-made substance on the ball. And even if he didn't, he had batters thinking about it—advantage Whitey in the mind game that takes place between pitcher and batter. Ford was held back a bit in the 1950s by his manger Casey Stengel who liked to save him for upcoming series against the better teams. But when Ralph Houk took over the club in 1961 he unleashed Whitey, letting him pitch every fourth day, and he dominated the American League going 25–4.

Leading off for the National League was Granville "Granny" Hamner, a shortstop with decent power for the Philadelphia Phillies, appearing in his third straight All Star game and playing second base in this contest. A teenager when he made his major league debut for the Phillies 10 years earlier, he became their full-time shortstop in 1948. He was a member of the Phillies' 1950, "Whiz Kids" team of young players that came out of nowhere to win the team's first pennant in 35 years—literally on a 10th inning home run on the last day of the season—and a team the City of Brotherly Love fell madly in love with. The "Kids" youth showed in the World Series when the Yankees dispatched them in four games. But they became an indelible part of Philadelphia baseball lore.

Granny would play virtually his entire career for the Phillies, save for stops in Cleveland and Kansas City, and did some managing in the Phillies farm system in the 1970s and 1980s. He died suddenly in a hotel room in 1993 in his beloved Philadelphia while attending a sports memorabilia show. Despite the passage of more than four decades, news stories and obituaries of his death referred to him as "Whiz Kids Shortstop" Granny Hamner.

Batting second was New York Giants' shortstop Alvin Dark. Born in Louisiana, he was standout baseball and football player in that state, quarterbacking the 1943, University of Louisiana-Lafayette team to an undefeated season and a New Year's Day victory in the Oil Bowl. After serving in World War II, he came home to play baseball, joining the Boston Braves and was part of that team's surprising run to the 1948 National League pennant.

He was traded to the New York Giants after the 1949 season, a swap that turned out to be one of the best in Giants' history as he was just rounding into All Star form; a gold-glove-caliber shortstop who could hit for power. He would play for a total of five National League teams before retiring in 1960 and begin a managerial career marked by peaks and valleys. He won the National League pennant with the now San Francisco Giants in 1962, but barely survived a 1964 controversy when he made racially charged remarks to a newspaper, a misquote, he claimed. Both Jackie Robinson and Willie Mays came to his defense, Mays having played with him as a teammate and under him as a manager.

After his stint with the Giants, he went on to manage the Kansas City Athletics then came to Cleveland in 1968, where crowds the size he would play in front of this day were rare indeed. He managed a third place finish that year and was given the additional duty of general manager the following year. He was now in the ultimately doomed position of negotiating puny contracts on behalf of cash-strapped Indians' owners with players he was, at the same time, trying to motivate on the field.

Fired in 1971 with the Tribe in last place, he was rehired by Finley in 1974 to manage the now Oakland Athletics, a high-flying bunch who were coming off consecutive World Series victories, and steered them to the American league pennant—becoming only the third manager at the time to win pennants in both leagues—and to a third straight World Series victory. He would manage briefly in San Diego in 1977 before retiring, but was not forgotten by Giants' fans who voted him the best shortstop in team history.

Batting third for the National League was Duke Snider of the Brooklyn Dodgers, playing in his fifth of what would be seven consecutive All Star games and leading the majors with a lofty, .367 batting average. On Opening Day 6 years earlier, Edwin Donald Snider was not in Brooklyn but in chilly Montreal where the talented, muscular, but free-swinging youngster took batting practice for the minor league Royals, under orders to watch pitch after pitch go by, until the strike zone became ingrained on his brain.

The lessons were not lost and before that year was over, he was called up to Brooklyn and would not look back. There, the slugging centerfielder would become the "Duke of Flatbush," for the neighborhood where the Dodgers played and where many of their fans lived and loved their team. Before it was shortened, the team was known as the Trolley Dodgers, a dismissive term sophisticated New Yorkers sniffed toward blue-collar Brooklyn with its trolley track-lined streets, but a delightfully urban team name if ever there was one.

The Giants and Yankees might have belonged to the city of New York but the Dodgers belonged to the neighborhoods of Brooklyn where many fans walked to games. They were affectionately known as the "bums," a nickname sometimes preceded by "dem." But to the Dodger's often critical but wildly loyal fans, dem bums were *their* bums, period. Playing in cozy, intimate Ebbets Field where players and fans could hear each other's conversations, the Dodgers had not won a World Series in team history, in woeful contrast to the 20 combined world titles of the Yankees and Giants going into 1954.

And nothing seared pain on the Dodger fan psyche more than the 1951 collapse when the team blew a seemingly insurmountable 13-game lead in August, and were caught on the last day of the season by their bitter crosstown rivals, the Giants forcing a three-game playoff for the pennant. After splitting the first two games, the Dodgers led 4–1 in the bottom of the ninth inning of game three at the Polo Grounds, the Giants home field, only to lose on Bobby Thomson's "shot heard 'round the world" home run in what, all things considered, must have been the most singular moment of sports fan agony in American history.

Normally cool Giants radio announcer Russ Hodges absolutely erupted:

"Branca throws. There's a long drive. It's gonna be, I believe—The Giants win the pennant! The Giants win the pennant! The Giants win the pennant! The Giants win the pennant! Bobby Thomson hits it into the lower deck of the left field stands! The Giants win the pennant! And they're going crazy! They're going crazy!"

In the losing clubhouse, Dodgers pitcher Ralph Branca laid face down and wept. Legendary sportswriter Red Smith, then of the *New York Herald Tribune*, wrote, "The art of fiction is dead. Reality has strangled invention. Only the utterly impossible, the inexpressibly fantastic, can ever be plausible again."

The Dodgers bounced back, winning the National League pennant in both 1952 and 1953, though losing both World Series to the Yankees. And with a total of six All Stars on the 1954 National League roster, the most of any club, Dodgers fans could feel that first Series win inching ever closer. Adding urgency to the matter were stories like the one in this day's *Plain Dealer*, "Dodgers Deny Plan to Move," regarding a possible move to Dallas. Team owner Walter O'Malley told the *Plain Dealer* reporter that he knew of no good reason for anyone to believe that the Brooklyn franchise was available. At least not yet.

O'Malley had muscled his way to sole ownership 1950, squeezing out Branch Rickey, the team president who had brought Jackie Robinson to the major leagues. An unsentimental, bottom-line first man, rumors of the beloved bums leaving had popped up before, talk most Dodgers fans simply refused to believe. And when the Dodgers finally won their first World Series the following year in 1955, the delirious, dancing Dodger fans parading down Flatbush Avenue would have sooner expected to see an alien spaceship land in Ebbets Field than for it to sit dark, empty, and awaiting the wrecking ball.

The Dodgers won the pennant again in 1956, giving them four flags and a Series win in five seasons and attendance was good. However Walter O'Malley wanted a new stadium, but on his terms only, something the New York powers that be were not going to give him. Rumors swirled through 1957 season that the team was leaving and frantic Dodger fans inundated Brooklyn's Borough Hall with telegrams and letters and rallied on its steps. An unmoved O'Malley moved the team anyway, taking the profitable club to eventual greater profits in Los Angeles, the hole he ripped in Brooklyn's soul of trifling concern to him.

After 75 years, the Brooklyn Dodgers were no more and many grieving Brooklyn fans never followed the game of baseball again. The dark joke that was told there for years afterward probably summed up Dodger fan's feelings as well as anything else: "Say you're in a room with a gun with two bullets and Adolph Hitler, Joseph Stalin, and Walter O'Malley, who do you shoot? Easy. You shoot O'Malley, twice."

In recent years, there have been revisionist versions of events faulting the city of New York for the Dodgers exit and painting O'Malley as an unwilling, even helpless, victim of circumstance. The same has also occurred, to a lesser extent, regarding another infamous franchise move—that of the Cleveland Browns whose owner, Art Modell, signed a deal in secret to rip the Browns from the city in 1995, a move felt in Cleveland like an appendectomy without anesthesia. The reality is that both were intelligent, ambitious men of wealth and free will who knew exactly what they wanted to do. And both went ahead and did exactly that.

In the top of the first inning, Whitey Ford had an easy time of it as Granny Hamner flew out to right, Alvin Dark fouled out to the shortstop and Duke Snider flew out to short left field. Score: National League 0, American League coming to bat.

What you don't know can't hurt you, or maybe it can. On this All Star Tuesday was an ad in the *Plain Dealer* for a carefree, hands-off bug killer for use around the home. "Murder for Bugs" touted the ad, and all one had to do "slip one of these lindane asbestos collars onto any light bulb, turn it on and lindane vapors pour swiftly into every crevice. Then it's good-bye flies, roaches ants, moths, mosquitoes, etc. throughout the room. Residual effect keeps house bug-free for weeks." Available by mail order from Chicago for $1.98.

The thinking on the powerful pesticide lindane has changed dramatically since that blissfully, or dangerously, ignorant day in 1954. It has been banned completely in more than 50 countries and has been barred from agricultural and veterinary use in the United States. Its remaining use in the United States is as a second line treatment for severe infestations of lice and scabies, in the form of a carefully applied lotion or a shampoo, when the preferred methods of treating these infestations fail. The days of breathing lindane vapors while sitting in the living room and reading the newspaper are, fortunately, in the past.

Taking the mound for the National League in the bottom of the first inning was Philadelphia Phillies right-hander Robin Roberts, the most dominant pitcher in baseball in the first half of the 1950s. He won 20 games in the Phillies 1950 "Whiz Kids" season, pitching well in, but losing, his only World Series start against the Yankees. It would be the only World Series game in which he would ever pitch. He would go on to win 20 or more games in the next 5 consecutive seasons, including a stellar 28–7 mark in 1952. A workhorse, he would lead the National League in innings pitched four straight seasons and at one point, seemed to be a sure bet to reach the coveted 300 career-win mark. He fell just short at 286—remarkable—considering he usually pitched for second division teams. He was inducted into the Hall of Fame in 1976.

Leading off for the American League was Chicago White Sox outfielder Saturnino Orestes Armas Minoso Arietta, better known to generations of baseball fans as Minnie Minoso. Born in Havana, Cuba, the dark-skinned Minoso was initially forced to play in the Negro Leagues before the major league race barrier fell; lighter-skinned Cuban players were allowed to play in the majors decades earlier. He broke in with Cleveland in 1949 before being traded to Chicago where he would spend most of his career and where he remains a beloved figure.

Athletes in any sport want to play as long as possible but Minnie's plan was simply to play forever. He is one of only two players to play in the major leagues in five decades (1940s–1980s) and with token appearances in 1993 and 2003 with the minor league St. Paul Saints, he played professionally in seven decades. The latter two appearances could be characterized as stunts, but they testify to both his longevity and love for the game. And he will be represented in baseball for a long time to come as in the concourse above left-center field in the White

Sox stadium stands a life-sized statue of him. At the 2004 unveiling, a tearful Minnie hugged his likeness and said, "If God takes me tomorrow, I'm happy …"

Batting second was Cleveland Indians second baseman Bobby Avila. Born Roberto Francisco Avila Gonzalez in Veracruz, Mexico, he would play virtually his entire career for Cleveland and remains one of the most popular players in team history. Despite playing most of the 1954 season with a broken thumb, he battled Minnie Minoso and Ted Williams to the wire for the American League batting title, edging both out to win the crown with .341 average. No Cleveland Indian has won a batting title since. After his baseball career, he served as mayor of Veracruz and later, president of the Mexican Baseball League and is credited with catalyzing the development of Mexican baseball.

Batting third for the American League was a young outfielder for the New York Yankees named Mickey Mantle. A generation of baseball fans grew up idolizing "the Mick," a fleet centerfielder who could hit long home runs and for high average from both sides of the plate. The icon he replaced in the Yankee outfield, Joe DiMaggio, called him "the greatest prospect I can remember."

In his 1951 rookie season, Mantle played along side of DiMaggio and both converged on a Willie Mays fly ball in the World Series that year. DiMaggio called for the ball at the last second and when Mickey pulled up, he caught his cleats on a drain cover, tearing up his right knee. He was carried from the field on a stretcher, one of a series of injuries that would plague his career, leaving many to wonder what he might have accomplished with a healthy body. Off the field, alcohol affected his playing career, family life, and eventually his health, something he profoundly regretted in his latter days, and a subject of which almost as much has been made of as what he did on the field.

However in an era when baseball was America's premier sport, before ball players were multi-millionaires, and when the media seldom reported the details of an athlete's personal shortcomings, Mickey was a genuine American hero. And, unlike dominant players like Babe Ruth and Joe DiMaggio who came before him, Mantle burst on the baseball scene just as television did. People all over the country were seeing black and white images of players like him up close in their living rooms for the first time.

The Yankees, in particular, were a favorite for the Saturday afternoon Game of the Week broadcasts and there would be Mickey at the plate with that smooth but powerful swing that looked like he wanted to hit the ball to Long Island, who would then in the outfield, gracefully run down a 400-foot plus blast to the chasm that was the old Yankee Stadium centerfield.

Across America in the 1950s and 1960s, countless boys in countless towns trotted to centerfield on soft and golden summer days and once there, they peered into the diamond, pawed the turf, pounded their glove, adjusted their caps, and they were Mickey Mantle. And that weedy, sun-baked ground where they were standing was not the neighborhood ball field but the plush, green grass of Yankee Stadium. The P. F. Flyer sneakers and torn jeans they were wearing were cleats and Yankee pinstripes.

Mickey was born in 1931 in a dusty Oklahoma small town during the grip of the Great Depression. His lead and zinc miner father Mutt Mantle dreamed of his son playing major league baseball someday and pushed him furiously in that direction. As much as he wanted baseball for Mickey he was also driven by what he didn't want; for his son to choke on dust in the mines every day like he did and die young like he would. The boy he drilled for hundreds and hundreds of hours turned out to be a better ballplayer than he ever dreamed, very little of which he got to see. Although this was only Mickey's third All Star game, Mutt Mantle had already been dead for 2 years.

In 1956, Mickey won the elusive Triple Crown, leading the American League in home runs, runs batted in, and batting average. Only two players have done it since in either league. After a solid 1957 season, his batting average was 12 points higher than in 1956, and Yankees General Manager George Weiss offered him a $17,000 pay cut telling him, "That's all you're worth." Baseball player's salaries today may be extravagant, but they weren't always.

Batting fourth for the American League was a major cog in the World Series winning machine that was the New York Yankees going into 1954, catcher Yogi Berra. A kid from an Italian neighborhood of St. Louis known as "the Hill," his immigrant father—the mirror opposite of Mickey Mantle's—was baffled and even disturbed by his boy's interest in baseball which he considered to be a "bum's game."

He signed a minor league contract with the Yankees in 1942 and 2 years later on the morning of June 6, 1944, was a sailor in a squadron of small rocket boats assigned to draw near and spray Omaha Beach with rocket fire in advance of the massive D-Day invasion to immediately follow. Berra's ship was able to fire its rockets and escape despite murderous German gunfire; Yogi and his mates escaped drowning a few days later when their boat was swamped in a storm.

After the war, he played briefly in the minors before joining the Yankees in 1947 and became the Yankee's full-time catcher in 1949, the first of what would be five consecutive World Series title years. Blessed with excellent bat control, in 1950 he struck out a miniscule 12 times in 597 at bats; players have been known to strike out that many times in a week.

In 1952, he became the first catcher to hit 30 home runs in a season and won the American League's Most Valuable Player (MVP) Award, his first of what would be three MVP awards, not just for his offense but for his fine defensive work and skill at handling pitchers. His knowledge of the game and overall reliability led Yankee Manager Casey Stengel to refer to him as, "Mr. Berra, my assistant manager." In later years, Yogi would manage both the Yankees and the Mets, winning a pennant in each league.

As much as fans liked Yogi Berra the ballplayer, they both liked and related to the person as much or more. Stocky, with a bit of a catcher's mitt for a face, he didn't look like the prototypical athlete and his malapropisms, or "Yogi-isms" will long outlive him. Baseball, he once observed, "is 90 percent mental. The other half is physical." His seemingly redundant, but maybe not so, observation, "It's déjà vu all over again" has found a place in American phraseology. And in 1956, when named vice-president of the Yoo-Hoo Chocolate Soft Drink Company, a woman asked if Yoo-Hoo was hyphenated. "No, Maam, he offered by way of sincere explanation, "it isn't even carbonated."

Batting fifth for the American League was Cleveland Indians first baseman Al Rosen, a slugger who played his entire 10-year career with Cleveland. Coming off a monster year in 1953 when he won the American League's Most Valuable Player award, he missed winning the Triple Crown by one percentage point on his batting average. Known as the "Hebrew Hammer," he is considered to be one of baseball's best all-time Jewish players and one who carried his heritage proudly and defiantly, challenging a number of players to fights when they insulted his ancestry. Once he was established as a star, he considered changing his name to something more Jewish-sounding such as Rosenstein so there would be no mistake about who he was.

But it was not ethnic issues on Rosen's mind this All Star day but a terribly sore right index finger that kept him awake most of the night with worry that he wouldn't be able to perform well in the big game in front of the hometown crowd. After a painful batting practice, he told AL Manager Casey Stengel to take him out anytime he'd like, that he didn't want to let the team down or be "the All Star game goat" as he told the *Plain Dealer*.

In the bottom of the first inning, Minnie Minoso flew out to deep center field and Bobby Avila bounced single through the hole between short and third. Mickey Mantle flew out to shallow center field and Yogi Berra walked on five pitches. Al Rosen came to the plate with two on and his fears were realized as he struck out weakly on three pitches to end the inning. Rosen looked over at Stengel but Casey had no intention of taking him out. Score: National League 0, American League 0 at the end of the first inning.

Back in Bobby Avila's native Mexico this day, death stilled the fiery spirit of the painter Frida Kahlo. Her obituary was carried in many U.S. newspapers the following day, mentioned as much for her marriage to famed Mexican muralist Diego Rivera than for work of her own. Yet like many artists, renown would come in death rather than in life. And like many artists, her work was fueled by personal pain and suffering.

Kahlo was a precocious 18-year-old in 1925, a childhood bout with polio leaving a leg slightly withered but her spirit intact. She had ambitions to be a doctor, bold plans in conservative, Catholic Mexico where gender roles were even more defined than in the United States. Her life was changed forever on a rainy September day when the bus she was riding on was demolished in a collision with a trolley car. The accident killed several passengers shattered bones in Kahlo's body, literally from head to toe, and left a horrific wound in her midsection when she was impaled by an iron railing. She was not expected to live the night.

But she refused to die and what followed was a year of grueling recovery marked by surgeries, plaster casts and pain, pain that would follow her the rest of her life. Her injuries would also prevent her from having children, to her great sorrow. It was during her convalescence that she began to paint, favoring bold and bright colors, many done while recovering from the 30-plus surgeries that would shadow her days. Many of her images were graphic and disturbing, such as the image of her own head on the body of a running deer shot with multiple arrows, as she was pierced so many times in her accident and on the operating table. Some considered her work to be surrealism, a label she rejected, explaining, "I paint my own reality."

Her marriage to Rivera was stormy—they divorced early in 1940 and remarried before the year was out—but it exposed her to art world luminaries in the United States and Europe; and she had exhibitions in New York and Paris. As the decade progressed she produced some of her best work, despite pain as a constant companion, and did some teaching as well. In 1953, she was virtually bedridden, facing amputation of a gangrenous leg and was dependent on painkillers and alcohol; she once remarked, "I tried to drown my sorrows but the bastards learned how to swim." In April of that year she had her first solo show in Mexico City despite being bedbound; she had her great, four-poster bed hauled to the gallery and the crowd, seeing her work together in a major collection, was awed. But her physical decline continued and death overtook her at the age of 47 on July 13, 1954.

When she died she was not very well known outside of Mexico until the 1970s when her work began to garner international recognition. Women in particular were drawn not only to her art but to her life story and struggles. She has subsequently been the subject of books, plays, and movies; the film Frida was nominated for six Oscars, winning two. And in 2001 she became the first Hispanic woman ever to be honored with a U.S. postage stamp.

In the sports pages of the *Pittsburgh Post-Gazette* was a wire story that barely hinted at the much larger things that would come. "Major League Players Band Together" told of the birth of the Major League Baseball Players Association (MLBPA) the day before when representatives from each team, meeting in Cleveland, voted to organize. They were a bit sheepish about it at first, as their attorney/spokesman, denied that the player's action could be construed as the forming of a union. This reluctance would not last long.

The largely toothless MLBPA began to cut its teeth in 1966 when it hired Marvin Miller, a tough, shrewd economist, as its head. In 1968, he negotiated the first Collective Bargaining Agreement ever among professional athletes and the union began to grow fangs. In 1975 baseball's "reserve clause," which bound a player to his team for life, was overturned and players could offer their services to the highest bidder—players' salaries soared. Tensions increased over the years between players and owners, or the rich and the very rich and labor negotiations grew into a war. In August 1994, the players walked out and wealthy men on both sides pouted as stadiums across the country fell dark and silent. They stayed dark and October passed with no playoffs or World Series as fans across the country just shook their heads.

Second Inning

Leading off the second inning and batting fourth for the National League was St. Louis Cardinal outfielder Stan Musial who played his entire 22-year career for St. Louis, something unheard of in today's game, and was a 24-time All Star selection. Baseball had two annual All Star games for a short period. A great and incredibly consistent hitter, he finished his career with 3,630 hits: 1,815 at home and 1,815 on the road. A well-regarded gentleman both on and off the field, a statue of him St. Louis erected outside the stadium after he retired was inscribed simply, "Here stands baseball's perfect warrior. Here stands baseball's perfect knight." Sometimes 10 words can say ten thousand.

Initially a rising young pitcher and outfielder in the Cardinals minor league system, a shoulder injury to his pitching arm toward the end of the 1940 season sent him to the outfield for good. He was called "Stan the Man," a nickname that came not from the hometown Cardinal fans but from the denizens of hitter-friendly Ebbets Field in Brooklyn where he regularly lined shots off and over its walls. Musial would come to bat there and the fans would groan something along the lines of, "here comes that man again." A St. Louis sportswriter picked up on it and the name stuck.

Batting fifth was Cincinnati Reds first baseman Ted Kluszewski, playing in his second of four consecutive All Star games. "Big Klu," as he was known in the city on the banks of the Ohio River, was one of the most powerful baseball players ever with biceps and shoulders that ripped the stitching out of an ordinary jersey. But this did not prevent him for being a graceful fielder, leading National League first basemen in fielding percentage for five consecutive years (1951–1955), a major league record. He was having a banner year in 1954 and would win the National League RBI title with 141. A 10-year player for the Reds and one of the more popular players in team history, he finished his career with several other teams, injuries slowing down his later years.★

Batting sixth was St. Louis Cardinal third baseman Ray Jablonski who, in sharp contrast to teammate Stan Musial, was making his only All Star game appearance. He played for five teams in an 8-year major league career, his peak years coming in 1953 and 1954 when he drove in more than 100 runs in each. He was a favorite of the fans in old Sportsman's Park in St. Louis who would chant "Go, Go Jabbo" when he came to the plate. Unlike Ted Kluszewski, fielding bedeviled him, as he led the league in errors in 1954 with 34.

In the top of the second, Whitey Ford continued to pitch well as Stan Musial singled in front of a diving Hank Bauer in right field, Ted Kluszewski grounded into a double play, and Ray Jablonski grounded out to short. Score: National League 0, American League 0, in the middle of the second inning.

In steamy Detroit where the temperature hit 97 degrees this Tuesday, murder also dominated the front page. Unlike the one in Cleveland,

---

★ Technically, Kluszewski was playing for the Redlegs as the team had changed its name from the Reds the previous year, a name they'd played under since 1890. The anticommunist sentiment and, at times, hysteria of the era produced not only a legitimate fear of communism but as great a fear of being labeled as sympathetic to that cause, even through something as innocent as the name of a baseball team. Common sense returned in 1958 when the team went back to being the Reds, which is how the team will be referred to in this book.

this one was far less mysterious. The previous Memorial Day weekend, a prominent Detroit dentist strode into a swank Lake Michigan summer home where a group of friends were playing gin rummy. Among the players were his wife and a purported industrialist from New York he believed to be her lover. Seconds later the New York man lay dead with a pair of gunshot wounds, including one through the heart, while a woman's voice screamed, "Why didn't you kill me?"

The doctor walked out of the house twirling a gun on his finger and told a thoroughly startled gardener, "I've done my job. He isn't going to take anyone else's wife. I've seen to that," then handed the gardener the still warm weapon.

The hottest thing going in the city's three newspapers on this scorching day was the trial of the dentist, underway in Allegan, Michigan. His guilt was not the issue but his mental state as he was pleading temporary insanity—he had shot the industrialist only twice because his gun had jammed. His wife, testifying on his behalf, freely admitted to the affair which his lawyer claimed made him briefly insane. "Take The Gun Away," blared the page one headline from the *Detroit Times*. A photo of the dentist's wife showed her on the witness stand wearing sunglasses, testifying only after the prosecution agreed to her request to remove the gun from her sight.

The *Times* reporter in the courtroom had a feel for the gravity and soap of the moment. The "mother of three sons, told from the witness stand of the swift-moving romance that led her Detroit dentist husband to shoot and kill her playboy, phony millionaire friend from New York City. Gentle tears began to flow, without sobs, when the romance that led to her marriage was discussed, but she refused a recess saying: **"I want to go on**." Women in the courtroom brushed their eyes in sympathy."

Perhaps some jurors were brushing their eyes as well when 3 days later, a divided jury found the good doctor not guilty by reason of insanity. The defense immediately began a legal fight to keep him from being committed to an "asylum," as they were then called, and by Monday, according to newspaper reports, the dentist and his wife were talking reconciliation. Ain't love, and a good lawyer, grand.

The *Detroit Times* was an afternoon daily and part of the Hearst chain of newspapers and lest there be any doubt, a photo of William Randolph Hearst appeared atop the editorial page. At one time he was head of the largest newspaper and magazine conglomerate in the world.

Colorful and controversial, Hearst was a man of strong, even passionate opinions and was not shy about using his newspapers to set a national agenda. A mysterious explosion destroyed the battleship Maine in the harbor in Havana, Cuba in 1898, a major factor in the ensuing Spanish-American War. Hearst is given varying degrees of blame, historians disagree on this, for goading the United States government into this war of dubious necessity. But his position on it was unambiguous as two days after the Maine explosion, his *New York Journal* ran the headline, "War? Sure!"

In the 1920s one in four Americans read a Hearst newspaper before losses suffered during the Great Depression chipped away at his empire. He died in 1951 and by the end of the decade, so had the *Detroit Times* as television exacted a toll on newspapers—afternoon and evening ones in particular. His legacy continues today in Hearst Corporation, one of the nation's largest media companies.

In the *Detroit Free Press*, there was good news for laid-off Packard Motor Car Co. employees as nearly 5,000 had been called back to work the previous day. Packard, once the largest luxury automobile manufacturer in the nation, had just acquired Studebaker in an attempt to jumpstart its sagging sales. "It will be good to be working again," said one worker. "I hope this Packard-Studebaker merger is as good as it sounds. I hope it means permanent work and work for more people."

There would be permanent work but it would be at General Motors, Ford, and Chrysler. They were emerging as "the Big Three" automakers in the country as smaller passenger car manufacturers such as Packard, Studebaker, Kaiser, and Willys were on their way out. Nash and Hudson had also merged earlier in the year and would hang on, as the American Motors Corporation, until 1987, never achieving the size or stature of the others.

The auto industry drove Detroit from a smallish, diverse manufacturing city with a population of less than 300,000 in 1900 to the fourth largest city in the country with a population of nearly 1.6 million in just 30 years. Massive plants were built during that period, such as Ford's sprawling, River Rouge complex that once employed as many as 90,000 and the Dodge Main plant where at one time 30,000 workers punched the clock every day. Detroit was truly the Motor City—not only of the country—but of the world. Connected to Detroit by an industrial umbilical cord were dozens of cities and towns in surrounding Great Lakes and Midwestern states that manufactured parts bound for the assembly lines of Detroit. It was said that if Detroit sneezed, the Midwest got pneumonia.

In a *Free Press* column called "The Town Crier," Mark Beltaire bemoaned the sometimes rude and boorish behavior of Americans while traveling abroad. "Folks who would be horrified at the mere idea of criticizing a neighbor's home or cuisine in his hearing are often the worst offenders. First of all, they assume nobody outside the United States speaks English. That must be one of the reasons they feel free to pan everything in sight in loud tones as soon as they put foot in a foreign land. They don't like the food, the plumbing is inadequate, transportation stinks, and some of their looks and phrases imply: "Why don't these foreigners go back where they came from?"

A few years down the road the phrase "The Ugly American," from the title of the 1958 political novel of the same name, would to come to be applied to such conduct. Beltaire, a one-time hockey writer for the *Free Press*, began The Town Crier in 1945 and wrote it for 35 years. He was called one of the newspaper's "best-loved chroniclers" at the time of his death in 2005.

And a *Free Press* photo slugged, "Slow Boat to Mackinac Straits" showed a powerful tugboat towing a barge laden with a massive caisson destined be the first in the Mackinac Bridge that would finally link Michigan's estranged upper and lower peninsulas. The boat was struggling mightily against the Detroit River current, making less than 2 miles per hour. The huge, 90-foot caisson was destined to go near the center of the span and was built in a shipyard in Toledo.

Separated by the churning blue waters of the Straits of Mackinac, Michigan's upper and lower tiers were linked only by ferry rides and ones that could require a 24-hour wait during busy times or be shut down completely by bad weather or ice. The graceful, 5-mile long Mackinac Bridge took 5 years to build and opened in 1957 as one of the greatest suspension bridges in the world. To the people of Michigan, however, the bridge became so much more than concrete, steel, and cables joining separated geographical areas of the state. The "Mighty Mac" is a Michigan icon and beloved by children of all ages, and one that every Labor Day, more than 60,000 people line up to walk over.

In baseball, the Detroit Tigers were languishing in the second division where they would spend much of the decade. However in the following one, the Tigers would play a unique role, one that transcended the field of play. Fires burned and blood spilled in the summer of 1967 as one of the worst race riots the country had ever seen raged in Detroit. Forty-three died, more than a thousand were injured, and hundreds of buildings were burned, and a city, which had already been retreating behind racial lines since a deadly 1943 race riot, retreated even more.

The 1968 baseball season dawned in doubt and fear. No one knew what another long, hot summer would bring. In the suburbs, whites were feeling apprehensive while in the city, blacks were feeling alienated. If ever a city needed a magnificent, unifying, and healing distraction, it was Detroit.

The 1968 Tigers were a talented, veteran club having finished just one game out of first place the previous year. They hit the ground running in April and kept going, often winning games with late-inning dramatics and for the people of the Motor City, the timing couldn't have been better. More than 2 million fans clicked through the turnstiles as the Tigers rolled over the American League with 103 wins, taking the pennant by 12 games, the last season before divisional play. They got down three games to one in the World Series to the favored St. Louis Cardinals and, like they did during the regular season, came storming back in dramatic fashion to prevail, and delirious Detroiters celebrated. More than 100,000 fans filled downtown streets and blacks and whites danced together and shared bottles of beer and wine. The next day, the huge headline in the *Free Press* said simply, "We Win!" If ever a city just needed "win" it was Detroit. If ever a city just needed a "we" it was Detroit.

On this All Star Tuesday a *Cleveland Plain Dealer* article carried the ominous headline, "Lindbergh Warns of Sudden Attack by Atom Missiles," referring to famed aviator, Charles A. Lindbergh. Lindbergh had electrified the world with his solo flight across the Atlantic Ocean in 1927 and returned to America a larger-than-life hero. In the years after his epic flight, he championed the cause of civil aviation and in 1932, endured the kidnapping and murder of his infant son, Charles Jr., and the massive media publicity the crime generated. He moved his family to Europe in 1935 and, now an Army Air Corps colonel, made several trips to Germany to evaluate that country's air force as Nazi power was on the rise.

On a 1938 trip Lindbergh was awarded, at Adolph Hitler's urging, the Cross of the German Eagle by Herman Goering, commander of the German Air Force or Luftwaffe, for his contributions to aviation; relations between the United States and Germany were cordial at the time. When Germany invaded Poland in September 1939, Lindbergh resigned his colonel's commission and became heavily involved in the "America First" movement that opposed any U.S. involvement in the war in Europe, becoming its most high-profile spokesman. Joseph Stalin and the Soviet Union presented a much greater threat to world stability than did Adolph Hitler and Nazi Germany, Lindbergh believed, and that the United States and Germany should ink a non-aggression pact.

During some of his speeches, Lindbergh made statements viewed by many critics as antisemitic and his acceptance of the German cross and refusal to disavow it in wake of that country's subsequent warmaking helped fuel those charges. The hero was now seen by many as Nazi sympathizer and even his hometown of Little Falls, Minnesota, removed his name from the town water tower.

Lindbergh spoke out against America's involvement in a European war up until the Japanese attack on Pearl Harbor in December 1941 then fell silent. He tried to rejoin the Army Air Corps but was blocked by President Franklin D. Roosevelt whom he had deeply angered. He worked during the war as a consultant on air force-related matters and in 1944, while in the Pacific theater working as a consultant for United Aircraft, actually flew about 50 combat missions against the Japanese despite his civilian status.

After Germany's surrender in May, 1945, Lindbergh was sent to there by United Aircraft to evaluate its airplanes and came eventually to Nordhausen, production site of Hitler's top secret and highly advanced V-2 rockets. There he saw the futuristic rockets and nearby, cremating ovens and piles of human ash and bones, the remains of the Jewish and other prisoners worked or starved to death making the rockets.

After the war, Lindbergh kept a somewhat lower profile. The seizing of Eastern Europe and the subsequent Cold War proved him right about the Soviets. But in light of the Holocaust and the massive war that ravaged the European continent—very wrong about Germany.

But 1954 had been a bit of a comeback year for him. He was awarded the Pulitzer Prize for his book, *The Spirit of St. Louis*, published the previous year, which described his trans-Atlantic journey, and President Dwight Eisenhower had appointed him a brigadier general in the Air Force reserve. He was again speaking out, this time against the Soviet Union and gave an ominous assessment of the United States' preparedness for a missile attack.

Lindbergh felt that under the current arrangement, the United States could be damaged by a large-scale, first-strike assault, and the country would be left unable to respond. He called for a widespread decentralization of the U.S. aerial fleet, "scattered over hundreds of bases, too many for an enemy to paralyze with a single blow. This requires … a fleet in being of the most modern aircraft able to take to the air with atom bombs within minutes after an alarm is sounded." Given the luxury of viewing subsequent years in retrospect, Lindbergh's warning would appear to have been a bit on the alarmist side. But his fears reflected those that ran through the American psyche; that in a time of virtually unprecedented prosperity and growth, unimaginable devastation and horror could descend upon the country with almost no warning.

Leading off the bottom of the second inning and batting sixth for the American League was Detroit Tiger third baseman Ray Boone. Boone surely was excited to be playing in his first of what would be two All Star games but could not have had any idea of the family precedent he was setting. Not only did his son Bob play in the major leagues but so did two of his grandsons—Brett and Aaron Boone—and all three were named to All Star teams making the Boones baseball's first, and thus far only, three-generation All Star family.

Batting seventh was New York Yankee outfielder Hank Bauer, a grizzled veteran of life before he was a major league baseball player. The youngest of nine children in East St. Louis, Illinois, his father lost a leg in a mill accident and Bauer was forced to wear clothes made from feed mill sacks when the money ran short. A good high school player, he played in the White Sox farm system afterward, then joined the Marine Corps shortly after Pearl Harbor. He fought in the bloody island campaigns in the Pacific theater and led a squad of 64 men at the Battle of Okinawa, only six of whom survived, including Hank, with a serious leg wound that sent him home.

After the war, he worked as a pipefitter when he ran into a Yankee scout in a bar who remembered him, and who signed him to a tryout. In only 2 years, he was with the 1948 Yankees to stay, getting there as much on grit and determination as on talent. Though not a spectacular player, he was a solid outfielder on the fine Yankee teams of the 1950s.

He was not afraid to get in the face of a teammate, once pinning Whitey Ford to the dugout wall and telling him, "Don't mess with my money," in reference to Whitey's late-night partying possibly affecting his pitching—Ford and his buddy Mickey Mantle believed it was impolite to go to a bar or lounge and not stay for awhile. And once he crawled on top of the Yankee dugout looking for a fan who yelled racial slurs at catcher Yankee, Elston Howard. He explained later, "Ellie's my friend." After his playing days, Bauer coached for the Kansas City A's, then the Baltimore Orioles where he was named manager in 1964. He led the 1966 team to their first World Series title, a four-game sweep over the favored Los Angeles Dodgers.

Batting eighth for the American League was Chicago White Sox shortstop Chico Carrasquel. The pride of his native Venezuela, in 1951, he was the first Latin American player to make a major league All Star team. He also was the first of what became a line of great Latin American shortstops to play for Chicago. Latin players were few back then and were expected by management to speak English, and if they couldn't, that was their problem.

Today interpreters are made readily available for non-English speaking players, be they from Latin America or, increasingly, from Asia. In 1952, Carrasquel played alongside Hector Rodriguez, a non-English speaking Cuban, who was the White Sox's third baseman that year. In one game, Rodriguez kept repeating "Chicago White Sox" over and over. Finally, an exasperated Carrasquel said to him, "Hector, please say something different." Rodriguez explained, "Chico, they want me to speak English, the only thing I know is 'Chicago White Sox.'"

In the bottom of the second, Ray Boone fouled out to first, Hank Bauer lined a single to left, and both Chico Carrasquel and pitcher Whitey Ford struck out, Chico swinging and Whitey looking. Score: National League 0, American League 0, after two innings.

On this All Star Tuesday, the front page of *The Cleveland Press* carried the first of a five-part of a Scripps-Howard series by Frederick Woltman, a New York reporter who'd won a Pulitzer Prize in 1947 for his work exposing communists in the United States. Woltman's focus in this series, which carried the headline, "The McCarthy Myth: Record Fails to Back Up Red 'Expose,'" was on the most visible anticommunist of the day—Wisconsin Senator Joseph McCarthy.

The controversial McCarthy had risen to prominence the previous few years, alleging widespread communist influence in various elements of the American body politic, in particular the State Department and U.S. Army, and using the new medium of television to do so. His allegations were long on accusation and short on substantiation and his roughhouse methods were controversial.

McCarthy was keenly aware of the ascendant capabilities of power and was an expert at wielding it. At the height of his influence in Washington, many in government were reluctant to express an opinion that was out of the mainstream or, more so, left of center. Even President Dwight D. Eisenhower, whose administration was repeatedly maligned by McCarthy as being soft or even friendly toward communism, was reluctant to take him on. Some who were bathed in the white, hot light of a McCarthy attack saw their reputations, and careers, destroyed and at least one committed suicide.

Earlier in the year, the Army–McCarthy hearings as they were known, were viewed by millions on television. The first ever nationally televised congressional inquiry gripped the country and went on for 36 days spread over nearly 2 months, wrapping up in mid-June. Representing the Army was not an intimidated government underling, but a seasoned Boston lawyer named Joseph Welch who calmly cut away at McCarthy's claims.

On the 30th day of the hearing, McCarthy accused Welch of having a young staffer in his private law office who was a communist sympathizer, repeatedly mentioning the young lawyer's name. The man in question, Fred Fisher had at one time belonged to an organization that had communist sympathies, which had nothing to do with the matter at hand.

The normally unflappable Welch erupted. "Until this moment, Senator, I think I never really gauged your cruelty or recklessness. Fred Fisher is starting what looks to be a brilliant career with us. Little did I dream you could be so reckless and so cruel as to do an injury to that lad. I fear he shall always bear a scar needlessly inflicted by you … Let us not assassinate this lad further, Senator. You have done enough. Have you no sense of decency, sir, at long last? Have you left no sense of decency?" The Senate gallery erupted in applause and when the hearings concluded, McCarthy was falling sharply in public opinion polls.

Frederick Woltman wrote that McCarthy was actually harming the cause of anticommunism and said this of his record: "It shows that by his excesses, his scare-head accusations that eventually evaporate, his thumb-in-the-eye tactics and his inevitable injection of partisan politics, whether aimed at Democrats or at critics within his own Republican Party, McCarthy has completely befogged a major issue of the day." Criticism of McCarthy would continue to mount and before the year was over, he would be censured by his Senate colleagues by a 67–22 vote, bringing to an end his reign of error. He drifted out of the national limelight and, always a hard-drinker, began drinking even harder. He died of liver failure in 1957.

Theatrical value aside, the Army–McCarthy hearings demonstrated conclusively that television and American politics and political fortunes were forever going to be inextricably linked. Television was able to present a dimension of Senator McCarthy to the American people that newspapers could not have. Television worked well for the senator in the short-term nature of an exposure such as a press conference. But the lengthy hearings gave the American people a prolonged look at him and they did not like what they saw.

Leading the evening television schedule this All Star Tuesday was "Make Room for Daddy," later renamed "The Danny Thomas Show," starring Danny Thomas. In the 9 P.M. time slot on ABC, it was in summer reruns after completing its first season. The show was one of the most popular of the 1950s and featured Thomas as a successful night club singer dealing with a variety of amusing predicaments while trying to balance the needs of career and family.

Like all the sitcoms of that era, it presented an idealized version of family life in America where homes were always nice and neat, families were wholesome and loved each other, problems were superficial and resolved at episode's end, and the characters were white with no visible ethnicity. Thomas, an Ohioan, was a bit of an exception to this as he was Lebanese and raised by his immigrant parents in Toledo, about 100 miles west of Cleveland. Born Amos Jacobs, he derived the Danny Thomas moniker for the first names of two of his brothers. He would go on to be a great philanthropist, establishing St. Jude Children's Research Hospital in Memphis in 1962.

Nearly 20 years after the debut of Make Room for Daddy came "MASH," a dark-edged comedy that dealt with much deeper themes including the horrors and morality of war. The series marked a sharp departure from comedies of the Thomas era and also featured an actor raised in Toledo by Lebanese immigrant parents, Jameel Farah who, as Jamie Farr, created the memorable character of Corporal Klinger. Both series ran for 11 years.

On this All Star Tuesday, the nation's first baseball fan President Dwight D. Eisenhower was in Washington attending to the more serious matters of state. He was in the second year of his presidency and things were going pretty well. The country was at peace, its economic engine was in overdrive, he was a popular figure who commanded respect, even from opponents, and he was no doubt enjoying the slide from power of Senator Joseph McCarthy. Eisenhower despised McCarthy but had always refused to take him on directly, something for which he was criticized, especially during the 1952 presidential campaign. However he'd maintained, "I will not get into the gutter with that guy."

That was Eisenhower's diplomatic, low-key, eye-on-the-big-picture style and one that served him well in Europe in World War II. There as Supreme Commander of the Allied Expeditionary Forces, he had to deal with not only Nazi Germany but a coalition of ally egos in leaders such as British Prime Minister Winston Churchill and the Soviet Union's Joseph Stalin, military men such as U.S. Army General George S. Patton, British Field Marshall Bernard Montgomery, and General Charles De Gaulle of France.

Montgomery, in particular, could be rude, even insulting, to Eisenhower who on one occasion patted him on his knee and reminded, "Steady, Monty. You can't speak to me like that. I'm your boss." Yet it was Montgomery who wrote of Eisenhower after the war, "He has the power of drawing the hearts of men towards him as a magnet attracts bits of metal." It was this power that allowed Eisenhower, who had never seen front line combat, to lead the multifaceted allied coalition to victory over Germany and bring the massive, brutal European war to its conclusion.

He turned down both partys' overtures to run for the White House in 1948, then somewhat reluctantly agreed to be the Republican candidate in 1952. His campaign's simple slogan, "I like Ike" worked, as much as anything, because people liked him. Even his 1952 and 1956 presidential and ideological opponent, Adlai Stevenson admitted, "I like Ike too."

On this day, the president liked his chances on his proposed Health Reinsurance Bill he had sent to the House of Representatives, his first foray into the politically charged arena of health care. The bill would have allowed the government to underwrite private health insurance companies in order that they broaden their coverage to the general public. A United Press wire story noted, "The House today was ready to vote on—and probably approve—President Eisenhower's $25,000,000 health reinsurance plan."

However the House sent it down in flames by an unexpectedly harsh vote of 238–134 with 75 of Eisenhower's fellow Republicans voting against. In a postmortem phone conversation with "Mrs. Hobby," (Health, Education and Welfare Secretary Oveta Culp Hobby, second ever female cabinet head) he was told the "people who wanted socialized medicine voted against it and the people who didn't want socialized medicine voted against it," as he recalled in his diaries. Eisenhower saw the Bill as a means of improving health care while staying out of socialized medicine and blamed the American Medical Association in part, and their congressional allies, for the defeat. He saw the loss as a defeat for the American people and said that those who voted against it "just don't understand what are the facts of American life."

The Bill was classic Eisenhower centrism and, perhaps still smarting over the House vote, wrote a letter, dated July 13, 1954, expounding his philosophy to and old friend, General B. G. Chynoweth. He had served with the general in Panama 30 years earlier and there they once enjoyed the philosophical joust. In his note he talked about his philosophy of the "Middle Way."

He expressed frustration with people who see government as the solution to everything and who "knowingly or unknowingly are trying to put us on the path toward socialism. At the other extreme we have the people—and I know quite a number of them—who want to eliminate everything that the federal government has ever done that, in one way or another, represents what is generally classified as social advance … when I refer to the Middle Way, I merely mean the middle way as it represents a practical working basis between extremists, both of whose doctrines I flatly reject."

Eisenhower concluded his letter recalling Mark Twain's observation that, "All generalizations are false, including this one," then went on to make his own: "Excluding the field of moral values, anything that affects or is proposed for masses of humans is wrong if the position it seeks is at either end of possible argument."

Also in Washington, government was grinding along as a Senate banking committee had planned to refer two New Jersey builders, and the conflicting testimony they gave, to the Justice Department for possible perjury action. However plans hit a snag, and an embarrassing one at that, when a review of the transcript revealed that the builders were never properly sworn. No oath—ergo no perjury.

Third Inning

Leading off the third inning and batting seventh for the National League was outfielder Jackie Robinson who 7 years earlier broke the color barrier when he took the field for the Brooklyn Dodgers. The first black player ever to play major league baseball was Moses Fleetwood Walker in 1884, a catcher for the Toledo Blue Stockings of the American Association (AA), the AA was considered a major league then. His brother William also played on that Blue Stocking team.

When the-then minor league Toledo team played the Chicago White Stockings in an exhibition game the previous year, their star player, Cap Anson, saw Walker, an articulate and college-educated son of a physician, and shouted, "Get that nigger off the field!" Anson, who is in the Hall of Fame and who was perhaps the best player of the 1800s, was also a racist and would not let the issue go. He carried a lot of influence, and, along with others, exerted pressure on the powers that be—by the end of the 1887 season, the color line had been drawn—one that would stand 60 years.

Those six decades passed and on April 15, 1947, rookie Jackie Robinson strode to home plate on Opening Day in Ebbets Field and stepped over that line. The pressure on him was staggering. Not only did he have to perform at an elevated level, he had to do so while blocking out the hostility that would be coming his way, be it a snub from teammate, racial slurs shouted by opposing players and fans in the stands, or the death threats directed at him that began before the season even started.

Dodgers President Branch Rickey had long conversations with Jackie about this prior to bringing him up to the majors—that to react, to lose his temper and go after an abusive player or fan even though they richly deserved it, would be to give in to those who wanted him to fail. For he was not only carrying his own hopes and dreams, he was carrying those of Negro League players and about 14 million African-American citizens. And he had to do all this while in the role of a rookie trying to prove he belonged in the major leagues, pressure enough by itself. Jackie Robinson not only had to be an exceptional athlete, he had to be an exceptional human being as well.

In the end he proved to be both, but it wasn't easy early on. The Dodgers played a three-game series later in April against Philadelphia and their manager, Ben Chapman, an old Yankee who once played in the same outfield with Babe Ruth. Chapman was also an old racist who hated blacks, didn't like rookies, and Robinson was both—in the 1930s, Chapman taunted Jewish fans with Nazi salutes and antisemitic epithets.

At his direction, a torrent of vicious verbal abuse poured out of the Phillies dugout beginning in batting practice and continuing for all nine innings of all three games. It got so bad that during game three, Dodger second baseman Eddie Stanky, who initially said he would not play with a black teammate, bellowed toward the Phillies dugout, "Listen you yellow-bellied bastards why don't you yell at someone who can answer back!" When National League President Ford Frick later heard what the Phillies were up to, he ordered them to stop. The Dodgers played Philadelphia again in May and the now muffled Phillies, making a perverse play on the death threats Robinson had received, instead held their bats like rifles and aimed them at him.

In other incidents, players for both the St. Louis Cardinals and the Chicago Cubs, before their team's initial season series with Brooklyn, reportedly voted to strike rather than play because of Robinson's presence, although it's never been verified that actual strike votes took place. Regardless, Ford Frick stepped in and promised lengthy, even lifetime suspensions for anyone striking saying, "I don't care if it wrecks the National League for five years." The players got the message.

Ultimately, Robinson had no direct control over events exterior to him, although he could very much influence them by the way he played on the field. He had to swallow his rage and channel it into his game. He got off to a slow start in April and was playing an unfamiliar position at first base; he was much more comfortable at second base or in the outfield. Things got better in May and by June, he hit his stride, getting his average up to .300, stealing bases, beating out bunts, scoring runs and, in general, creating excitement. Fans in other cities were now coming out to see him and black fans were clicking the turnstiles in numbers not seen before. What's more, Brooklyn was breathing the rarified air of a pennant race and the Ebbets Field faithful were excited.

Led by Jackie, the Dodgers charged through the summer and in September clinched only their fourth pennant in club history. On September 12, he was named Rookie of the Year by *The Sporting News*, which had originally opposed the integration of baseball, and on the 23rd, he was celebrated with his own day at Ebbets Field and was given a 1947 Cadillac, a gold watch, and other gifts and cash, all bought with contributions from grateful Dodger fans. Three days later he was part of a team victory parade that drew more than a half a million to the streets of Brooklyn and received the loudest cheers when he was presented his rookie award at Brooklyn Borough Hall. It had been a remarkable year for Jackie Robinson. Although the brick wall of bigotry that stood before him when the season began was still there, he had, through sheer will, knocked a lot of those bricks out.

Batting eighth for the National League was one of the players who came through the door that Jackie Robinson opened, Dodger catcher Roy Campanella. In 1946 he, along with roommate Don Newcombe, were assigned to the Nashua, New Hampshire, Dodgers of the New England League, making the team the first racially integrated professional team of the twentieth century. There, he earned the confidence of Manger Walter Alston who designated him as his fill-in should Alston get tossed from a game. This happened in June, and Campanella became the first African-American to manage white players on a professional team, the Nashua club rallying from three runs down to win that game.

After winning the International League's Most Valuable Player (MVP) award with the Montreal Royals in 1947, Campanella was called up to the parent Brooklyn Dodgers for good in early July, 1948 where he quickly became the preeminent catcher in the National League in the manner that Yogi Berra was in the American, playing in eight consecutive All Star games starting in 1949. And, like Berra, he was one of a small group of players to have won three MVP awards, garnering the honor in 1951, 1953, and 1955. In 1953, he became the first catcher ever to hit 40 home runs, a record that stood until 1996. It was no coincidence that Campanella was behind the plate during Brooklyn's best years as a franchise.

Like all catchers, Campanella got beat up behind the plate and a series of injuries brought down his batting average in 1956 and 1957. He was hoping for a return to health for the following season with the Dodgers moving to Los Angeles and playing in the Coliseum there. With its very short and inviting left-field stands, it was a home run hitter's dream. But driving home early on a dark January morning in 1958, his car hit a patch of ice, clipped a pole, and overturned, hurling him under the dashboard. He tried to reach for the ignition and shut the engine off but his arms refused to move. He was paralyzed from the neck down.

More than 3,000 phone calls flooded the switchboard of *The New York Daily News* before the day was over, asking about Campanella's condition. But the news was grim; not only had Dodgers fans just lost their team—one their most popular players ever would never play or walk again.

All of Campanella's training and accomplishments as an athlete did not prepare him for what lay ahead; months and months of grueling physical therapy shadowed by his own personal bitterness and despair. It would be November before he could finally go home and continue therapy as an outpatient and through hard work, he regained much of the use of his arms although never was able to leave a wheelchair.

And he was able to regain his spirit as well and in 1959 wrote the inspirational book, *It's Good to be Alive.*

In the top of the third inning, Jackie Robinson grounded out to short and Roy Campanella fouled off five pitches to work a walk. Pitcher Robin Roberts unsuccessfully tried to bunt Campanella to second base where he was thrown out and Granny Hamner popped out to the shortstop as Whitey Ford continued in fine form. Score: National League 0, American League 0, in the middle of the third inning. The game, at this point, was bit of a pitcher's duel. This would not last long.

In the nations' capital, *The Washington Post* was enjoying a period of spectacular growth, having acquired the *Washington Times-Herald* earlier in the year to become the city's only morning newspaper, and was now dominating the District of Columbia's journalism scene. A cartoon on its Tuesday editorial page showed President Eisenhower, dressed as a ship's captain, being crowded away from the helm of the boat, which was inscribed "Foreign Policy," by a group of powerful senators. The frustrated president is asking, "Mind if I take a turn at it too?"

One of caricature senators doing the crowding was a bespectacled figure named Lyndon Baines Johnson, Democrat of Texas, who was largely unknown nationally and whose career would soon be seeing its own spectacular growth. In his first term as senator, he was already the youngest senate minority leader in history and in 6 months, with the change in Senate balance of power in the 1954 election, became the majority leader. A powerful man whose will prevailed like few in American political history, Johnson was the master of the hands-on, face-to-face conversation. He could literally pat you on the back or figuratively twist your arm behind it—occasionally at the same time.

He excelled at bringing a recalcitrant senator into his office and, looming his 6-foot, 4-inch frame over him, his face inches away, and telling him, with impassioned rhetoric and in impressive detail, why he should vote a certain way and making him feel as if the future of the republic hinged on his vote. Many a senator came from such a meeting suddenly seeing the world in L. B. J.'s light. Perhaps his greatest legislative achievement was guiding Eisenhower's Civil Rights Act of 1957 through the shoals of divided Democrats and oppositional Republicans. It was a fairly weak Bill, but it was the first civil rights law passed by the senate in 87 years and the precedent it set opened the door for stronger legislation down the road.

Unable to secure the 1960 Democratic Party presidential nomination, Johnson yielded to the rising star of John F. Kennedy (J. F. K.) and, somewhat surprisingly, accepted the role as his running mate. With J. F. K's victory in November, he assumed the largely ceremonial office of vice-president and began a trip to the back pages of American history as just another Washington powerbroker whose time had come and gone. This was violently and permanently altered when assassin's bullets cut down President Kennedy in Dallas on November 22, 1963. Power once again beckoned as L. B. J. took the presidential oath of office on Air Force One before it flew back to Washington. And when he landed, he was the never-nominated, never-elected president of a grieving United States of America.

In what have could have been a tumultuous final year of Kennedy's term was instead handled splendidly by L. B. J. He reached out to the American people as the humble caretaker of the late president's ideals and goals. He also kept Kennedy's people in place in the White House and in the cabinet, in effect reassuring the country that the bullets that flew in Texas did not reach Washington. For presidential candidate Johnson in 1964, the economy was relatively good and there were no real crises taking place as Viet Nam was a nightmare in waiting. The Republicans ran conservative Barry Goldwater who lacked widespread appeal and L.B.J. rolled to victory in the election with a record 61 percent of the vote. Ten years after appearing as a minor figure in a *Washington Post* editorial cartoon, he stood atop the American political mountain.

With a mandate firmly in hand, he embarked on a sweeping domestic policy agenda—a menagerie of ambitious social programs known as the Great Society. Johnson saw national and personal wealth not as ends in themselves but as means, "to elevate and enrich our national life" as he put it. Be it education, the environment, civil rights, poverty, or health care, there was no area in the president's view that couldn't be taken to unprecedented heights in a new and better world. What would fuel this was his belief, and one shared by the majority of the American people, that continued and increasing American affluence was inevitable, if not a birthright.

The confidence bordering on brashness the president brought to domestic matters he would also bring to foreign ones—Viet Nam, in particular. When he took the oath of office in 1965, The United States had about 23,000 troops or "advisors" in the country in what was then considered to be a police action. By the end of the year that number approached 200,000 in what had rapidly turned into a war of attrition.

Over the next 2 years, no amount of troops, bombs, or money seemed to be enough as military and civilian casualties continued to mount. Images of flag-covered coffins coming back to America and burning villages and civilian casualties in Viet Nam eroded Johnson's support at home and the cost of the war drained much of the funding life out of his Great Society. As discontent over the war grew, so did the angry and shrill chants of antiwar protestors. "Hey, hey L. B. J., how many kids did you kill today?" echoed through the streets of Washington and other American cities—cruel, haunting words from a nation divided. A man who wanted nothing more than to bring good things to people was being taunted as a killer.

In February 1968 alone, more than 700 U.S. soldiers were killed in Viet Nam and near the end of the month, trusted CBS news anchorman Walter Cronkite returned from a trip there and expressed his sincere doubts about the war at the end of a newscast. Johnson is reported to have said, "If I've lost Cronkite, I've lost Middle America." And on the last day of March, a haggard-looking Johnson stunned the nation when he announced he would not run for reelection that year. With nothing going right in Viet Nam and much of his Great Society dreams in tatters, he isolated himself to the White House for much of the rest of his term. Johnson, who frequently used the human female as a metaphorical vehicle, would later say, "… I left the woman I really loved—the Great Society—for that bitch of a war on the other side of the world …"

President Johnson's fall from the American political mountain was swift and complete. Although history will continue to judge him, it will be with the caveat, "if it hadn't been for Viet Nam …"

In the sports pages of *The Washington Post* was Sports Editor Shirley Povich and his column, "This Morning With Shirley Povich," one he would write longer than a lot of people live. A chance encounter as a teenaged golf caddy in his native Maine for the publisher of the *Post* in 1922 brought him to Washington as both a copy boy and the publisher's caddy. Two years later, Povich had his first sports byline and, too excited to wait for the first proofs to reach the newsroom, ran down to composing to run his fingers over the cold type of his name.

Povich would spend the rest of his life at the paper he loved, staying an astonishing 75 years writing both full-time and in semiretirement. Beloved as well by generations of Washingtonians, even death could not immediately stop him—his final column appearing the day after he died in 1998.

Povich brought a keen eye for what was happening on the fields of sport and his conscience as well; as early as 1939 he was critical of major league baseball for refusing to allow black players. And in 1953 he wrote a 13-part, prizewinning series on the subject titled, "No More Shutouts."

Povich's All Star break column this day analyzed the American League pennant race between the White Sox, the Indians, and the Yankees—New York having cut four games off of Cleveland's lead in just a week. After winning the American League 5 straight years, the Yanks were being seriously challenged.

The game was now nearing an hour in length on this hot day, and the concessionaires were busy—what would be a baseball game without some snacks, especially an All Star contest. Stadium menus were a little more basic then and on hand were 6 tons of hot dogs, 2 truckloads of ice cream, and enough soft drinks to fill more than 200,000 cups. In addition, there were 30,000 bags of peanuts, 15,000 bags of popcorn and 10,000 boxes of Cracker Jack, complete with surprise toy. And last, but not at all least, 175,000 bottles of beer were on ice—no sushi-serving wait staff at this ballpark.

The clang of sledge hammers on steel echoed across the Great Plains when the Northern Pacific Railroad (NPR), the first to cross the country's northern tier, rolled from its birth in the Great Lakes toward its Puget Sound destination near Seattle. It crossed the Missouri River in the Dakota Territory in 1872, and the hamlet there was named Edwinton after an NPR civil engineer. This was quickly changed to Bismarck, after German Chancellor Otto Von Bismarck, in hopes that immigrants from Deutschland headed west might stop and grow some roots. The idea obviously had merit because people of German ancestry are easily the number one group in modern-day Bismarck, North Dakota.

Eighty-two years after the founding of the city, the heat wave baking that northern tier and the All Star game in Cleveland were the top headlines running across *The Bismarck Tribune*. Hundreds of afternoon newspapers across the country splayed news of the game across the front page, even if the contest was incomplete at press time, in markets as large as Philadelphia, a city with two major league teams, and as small as Bismarck which was more than 800 miles from the nearest major league town. It was the golden age of baseball, not only in terms of the players on the field, but in the hearts and minds of Americans. With other major league sports in their comparative infancy, it was the common weave in the American family fabric, be it the sons and daughters of Bismarck Germans or those of the dozens of ethnic groups in Philadelphia, a city founded almost 200 years earlier.

In California this Tuesday, the *Long Beach Independent* told of the arrest of nine from the Long Beach area in a fraud broken up by the county sheriff Bunco Squad involving promotions giving away cash and cars at local theaters. The scam was relatively simple. Members of the group would linger near the theater stage waiting for a call for a volunteer to draw the winning ticket, hurry forward and offer their services, and then produce a ticket they had palmed. Nearly $10,000 in cash had been swindled in the past year while one member of the group admitted to "winning" nine automobiles since 1950. Drawing procedures were, presumably, tightened up in the aftermath.

The sports page featured a cartoon of a National League All Star watering the four-blossomed flower of four straight victories over the American League while gloating over the caricature of a hapless Casey Stengel who was watering a runt of a plant. In Pacific Coast League (PCL) standings, the Hollywood Stars were leading the eight-team league. Holding down the baseball fort in future major league cities were the Oakland Oaks, San Diego Padres, San Francisco Seals, Seattle Rainiers, and the Los Angeles Angels.

The PCL was known for its charming ball parks but perhaps none so much as Wrigley Field in Los Angeles. Built in 1925 by Angels and Chicago Cubs owner William Wrigley Jr., the striking stadium featured Spanish-style architecture, a 12-story office tower at its home plate entrance and, like Wrigley Field in Chicago, ivy-covered outfield walls.

The ballpark was also home to one of the PCL's most colorful characters, Lou "The Mad Russian" Novikoff, an outfielder who tore up the league in 1940, winning the Triple Crown and batting .363 with 41 home runs. He drove in 171 runs that year, a lofty 60 more than the runner-up. He did this while being "coached" by his wife, Esther, who sat in a home plate box seat and who booed and otherwise verbally abused him at every bat, doing so at her husband's instruction. Inspiration can come from different directions.

A poor outfielder, one writer said Novikoff wrestled balls to the ground more than he caught them; he once tried to blame his challenged fielding on a crooked left field foul line. Other Mad Russian legends include: a fear of ivy so great he would let catchable balls bounce off Wrigley's outfield wall; a game where he stole third base, despite the bases being loaded, because he had such a great jump on the pitcher that he just couldn't resist; and a pet Russian Wolfhound that accompanied him everywhere and ate only caviar. A lover of the nightlife, staying out till dawn was not uncommon and one roommate said, "I roomed with Lou's clothes."

He was brought up to the Chicago Cubs with great fanfare in 1941 and struggled both at the plate and with Wrigley Field's major league ivy until a Cubs trainer walked him out to the wall, took ivy leaves and rubbed them on his body and even chewed them to prove they were harmless, which seemed to help. Novikoff hit .300 in the war-thinned league in 1942, but before the war's end was back in the PCL, just another minor league slugger who didn't make it in the majors. It's more than a bit ironic that an ivy-phobic baseball player would play in what may have been the only two stadiums in America with ivy-covered walls.

The PCL, unlike the other two Triple-A leagues, the International League and the American Association, did not share territory with major league teams. Big-league baseball had yet to cross the Mississippi River which led to a sort of splendid isolation for the league and one in which it prospered. The west coast weather allowed teams to play longer seasons (the San Francisco Seals once played 220 games in a season) and pay competitive salaries and many major league caliber players, particularly ones from California, chose to stay in the PCL rather than move up to the bigs. And by 1952, the league was doing so well it was granted "open classification" status placing it above the IL and the AA and there was talk of making it a third major league. But all that ended when the Giants and Dodgers moved to the west coast in 1958.

The further expansion of major league baseball westward nearly killed the PCL but it bounced back. However in the more recent version of the league, only 3 of 16 teams actually play on the west coast, the rest scattered across the Midwest, South, and Southwest. Minor league baseball, as a whole, has had to reinvent itself to maintain its place in the American landscape.

In the bottom of the third inning for the American League, Minnie Minoso walked, Bobby Avila lined a single to left, Minoso stopping second, and Mickey Mantle struck out. Yogi Berra bounced a chopper to the first baseman who stepped on the bag, Minoso and Avila each moving up a base. Up to the plate came Al Rosen, his swollen and sore finger sticking straight out, who pitcher Robin Roberts had easily whiffed with two runners aboard in the first inning. He would later say the strikeout made him so angry, he sort of forgot about the finger. He slammed a Roberts fastball over the left-center field fence for a home run as a Hall of Fame outfield of Jackie Robinson, Duke Snider, and Stan Musial could only watch. The Cleveland crowd stood and roared and had barely quieted when Ray Boone homered in almost the exact same spot. Hank Bauer struck out as the inning came to a noisy end. Score: American League 4, National League 0, after three innings.

A brief piece in *The Cleveland Press* noted a recent study conducted by a major insurance group that daydreaming was responsible for 16 percent of all auto accidents: "Daydreaming behind a wheel often steers drivers to eternal sleep." Modern-day drivers now have cell phones and texting to keep them from daydreaming.

In Emmetsburg, Iowa in the northwest part of the state on this Tuesday, life had pretty much "ground to a halt as the breezeless, sticky weather caused the usual amount of discomfort," according to the weekly *Emmetsburg Reporter*. To make matters worse, a very wet spring and early summer combined had produced hordes of flies and mosquitoes leading the city council to declare "Operation Insect" where the town would be sprayed from the air with insecticide early the next two mornings. Residents were warned to cover their cars and fish ponds and to remove all laundry from clotheslines. No mention was made in the article of possible health risks from either breathing or having skin come in contact with the spray.

On America's west coast, communism was also a front and center issue, this time on page one of the *Los Angeles Times*. "Film Group Loses Red

Ouster Suit," was the headline at the top of the page. The suit was filed by 23 Hollywood actors and writers who claimed they had been denied employment, or been blacklisted by film studios after being subpoenaed the previous year by the House Un-American Activities Committee (HUAC) and had either refused to answer certain questions relating to alleged communist activities or refused to appear at all.

The suit was directed at 16 film studios as well as various film executives and distributors, as well as several members of HUAC. The Los Angeles Superior Court judge had thrown out the claims against the studios and executives but ruled that an amended, more explicit suit could yet be brought against the committee members.

HUAC was a standing committee of the House of Representatives that held a number of hearings during its existence to investigate the influence of communism on Hollywood's film industry including 1951-to-1952. Hundreds of writers and actors were called with many suffering varying degrees of consequent professional or personal damage if they were deemed to be "unfriendly." Even having your name merely mentioned during a hearing could have a negative impact.

Many incorrectly associate Senator Joseph McCarthy with HUAC who, as a member of the Senate, had no direct involvement. However both entities very much reflected the internal Cold War taking place in the country at the time. Arthur Miller's 1953 play, "The Crucible," while factually depicting the 1692 Salem witchcraft trials was, in reality, an allegory of HUAC and its activities. Miller himself was called before the committee in 1956 and, in a bit of payback, perhaps, convicted of contempt. His conviction was later reversed on appeal.

The threat communism represented to the United States and to the world at the time was genuine. However the committee's modus operandi—that of forcing American citizens to stand and quake before a powerful body out to determine if their personal views were "American" enough—was disturbing an increasing number of people. In 1959, former President Harry S. Truman called HUAC, "the most un-American thing in this country today." Its influence declined throughout the 1960s and it was abolished in 1975.

Also on page one of the *Times*, "Hunger-Striking Finn Twins' Appeal Delayed." George and Charles Finn were identical twin brothers who were in the third week of a hunger strike in the medical unit of federal prison in California. Their journey there began in 1952 when they purchased a surplus World War II transport plane from the California school district it had been donated to with the intent of starting their own airline, The Flying Finn Twins Airline. Both brothers were war veterans, Charles as a bomber pilot and George as a flight instructor.

However the government ruled that as donated war surplus, the plane could be used for educational purposes only and took it back. One of the brothers then stole the plane and flew it to a desert airstrip in Nevada. For a time, both brothers lived in their desert-bound airship, guarding it at gunpoint, and pleading their cause to anyone who would listen. This earned them a good deal of notoriety, including a story and photo spread in *Life* magazine, Charles standing on a wing with arms defiantly crossed—gun and holster on hip. They eventually were taken into custody and charged with theft but no indictment was handed down as a key witness could not identify which twin actually stole the plane.

Not willing to let it go, the indefatigable, or insane Finns upped the ante. With a photographer and radio broadcaster in tow they stopped and handcuffed a U.S. attorney on an Los Angeles (LA) street, calling it a "citizens' arrest" for violating their rights. The Feds were not amused. The duo was convicted in early June 1954 of conspiracy and assaulting a federal officer and sentenced to one year in prison. In this day's story, the twins were losing weight but otherwise reasonably healthy in their hunger strike and demanding their release on bail, their appeal being delayed a day by a busy appeals court docket. Their strike may have had some effect because they were released about 4 months into their sentence. In following years, they would battle the government on a variety of issues but never got their airline.

In sports, the All Star game would be starting in mid-morning on the West Coast and LA residents were eagerly awaiting it, according to *Times* television critic Cecil Smith. "This will be one of those mornings when the wheels of the city pause—and darned near stop turning. Offices not equipped with TV or radio will suddenly be vacated.

Saloons and restaurants will be packed." Smith went on to wax nostalgic about listening to one of the famous 1920s Jack Dempsey–Gene Tunney fights on the headphones of a crystal radio set and marveled that today's game could be watched live on television with the flick of a switch. "Man we've gone a long way in 30 years—we've really traveled." Smith, who had a long and respected career with the *Times*, would do more traveling than he could have imagined as he lived well into the Internet age, dying in 2009 at the age of 92.

Fourth Inning

Several new faces would enter the game in the top of the fourth inning including Chicago White Sox pitcher and native of Cuba Sandy Consuegra, taking over for Whitey Ford. In an 8-year career, Consuegra pitched primarily in relief and had one stellar year, 1954, in which he went 16–3 with the second lowest earned run average in the league and made his only All Star game appearance.

Also appearing for the American League was Cleveland Indians pitcher Bob Lemon, one of the best pitchers in the team's history and playing in his last of seven consecutive All Star games. His journey to the Hall of Fame was an odd one considering that on Opening Day 1946, he was not a pitcher at all but Cleveland's starting center fielder. He struggled at the plate and Cleveland Manager Lou Boudreau tried him in the bullpen where he found his niche.

By 1948, he was a full-time starter, winning 20 games in leading Cleveland to the World Series where he won 2 more. The Indians won that World Series and haven't tasted that wine since. He would also compile a 23–7 record in this All Star year helping Cleveland to the American League pennant. After retiring as a player, he would go on to have a long career scouting, coaching, and managing. His greatest success managing came with the Yankees, guiding them to the 1978 World Series title after taking over for Manager Billy Martin midway through the season. He would also manage the Yankees for parts of the 1979 and

1981 seasons, in the days when Yankees owner George Steinbrenner was conducting managerial musical chairs.

Appearing for the National League was Don Mueller, a slick-hitting outfielder who played 10 of his 12-year career with the New York Giants and was playing in his first of what would be 2 All Star games. His excellent bat control led teammates to call him "Mandrake the Magician." He played a pivotal but painful role in the Giants stunning 1951 National League (NL) playoff win over the Brooklyn Dodgers. He raced from first to third during the historic ninth-inning rally and ripped a tendon his ankle when he slid. The game was delayed while he was carried from the field on a stretcher while Bobby Thomson, and baseball history, waited on deck.

In the top of the fourth inning, Sandy Consuegra got Alvin Dark to fly out to center but it would be all downhill for Consuegra from there. Duke Snider singled to center, Stan Musial singled to right with Snider taking third, Ted Kluszewski bounced a single over the first baseman scoring Snider and sending Musial to third and Ray Jablonski singled to center, scoring Musial with Kluszewski stopping at second. Jackie Robinson then slammed a double off the right center field fence scoring both Kluszewski and Jablonski for the NL's fifth straight hit.

Casey Stengel by now had seen enough and Bob Lemon replaced Consuegra on the mound. Roy Campanella popped out to third and then Don Mueller, pinch-hitting for the pitcher Robin Roberts, doubled up the alley in right center field, scoring Robinson. The ninth man to bat in the inning, Granny Hamner, grounded out to third as the NL had come storming back. Score: National League 5, American League 4 in the middle of the fourth inning.

In stark contrast to the thrill and excitement of the game, a sad and somber scene was taking place on the lakeshore about 5 miles east of the stadium. The previous Sunday evening, 20-year-old lifeguard Thomas Hronek was swimming off a Lake Erie beach and disappeared. Some confusion followed. There was a report he might have been picked up by a passing motorboat, thus a search was not immediately ordered by authorities. Since that evening, the handsome young man with plans to enter the air force had not been seen or heard from.

On this Tuesday afternoon while other fathers and sons were at the game, Thomas's frantic and frustrated father and brother began the search themselves, borrowing dragging hooks from the fire department. When the sun had set, a day of what must have been physically and emotionally exhausting work produced nothing. The next day, the Coast Guard took over and his body was found floating in the water. The following Saturday, the Hronek family buried their Thomas.

Major league baseball had yet to come to Minneapolis in the summer of 1954 but the Millers of the International League were there and on this All Star Tuesday, the fans were still talking about the previous night's game. "The 2,025 fans that went to Nicollett Park Monday night saw quite a show—one of the greatest exhibitions of power pitching the old enclosure has ever witnessed and had it well flavored with rhubarb," wrote Bob Beebe of *The Minneapolis Star.*

The old enclosure had been built in 1896 and like so many long-gone stadiums, Nicollett Park had a character of its own—from its unique, Tudor architecture entry building with a deeply-pitched, Spanish, red-tile roof, to its intimate right field wall only 279 feet away that saw many hundreds of home runs scream over it, to its 6 P.M. Sunday game curfew. In a 1935 second game of a Sunday doubleheader, the Toledo Mud Hens rallied for five runs in the top of the ninth inning to take a 5–3 lead and Millers strolled to bat in bottom of the frame at 5:54 P.M. They hemmed, hawed, and stalled until the clock struck 6:00, the game ended, and the score reverted to the last full inning played, giving the Millers a 3–0 win.

The old enclosure had also seen plenty of arguments, or rhubarbs, but saw a good one Monday evening when the Millers' pitcher was tossed from that game for intentionally hitting, in the umpire's opinion, an Indianapolis Indians player. A *Star* photo showed incensed Millers Manager, Bill Rigney, shaking his finger under the ump's nose in vain protest.

Compared to other American sports, baseball has always had a different set of rules when it comes to managers protesting game officials' decisions. In-your-face yelling, arm-waving, dust-kicking, tobacco juice-coated cursing have always been tolerated providing the whole thing doesn't go too far, which is strictly the umpire's subjective call.

Such protests by coaches in other major league sports, especially delivered on the field of play, would get that coach ejected, fined, and quite possibly suspended by league officials. Yet in baseball, they're generally put up with and allowed to run their course, ending with the manager trotting back to the dugout and the fans laughing. Rigney, who later managed 18 years in the majors, was incensed because the "duster" that hit the batter, was a slider. And no self-respecting pitcher would dust a player with a slider or any other breaking pitch. It would be a fastball, usually aimed around the ribs.

And the old enclosure had seen plenty of dominating pitching performances and perhaps none quite so much as the one by a young, fireballing, Indianapolis Indian, left-hander named Herb Score. He had wowed the crowd with a complete game, six-hit shutout, while striking out 17 batters to run his record to 15–2. He would finish the year 22–5, his 330 strikeouts still an Indianapolis season record, but was never called up to parent team Cleveland as the big-league Indians had the best starting rotation in team history with three of five starters on their way to the Hall of Fame. However Score was there in 1955, winning Rookie of the Year honors and making the All Star team. An All Star again the next year, he was forging his own path to Cooperstown. Both Mickey Mantle and Yogi Berra would later say he was one of the best pitchers they ever faced.

But everything changed on a chilly May night in Cleveland in 1957 when a vicious line drive off the bat of the Yankees' Gil McDougald smashed into Score's right eye, shattering multiple bones in his face. He crumpled to the ground and Municipal Stadium went dead silent as the public address announcer asked if there was a doctor in the stands. Several rushed to the field but the damage had been done.

He would not pitch again that year and a distraught McDougald said he would retire if Score lost his vision. He got all his vision back, but never his dominance as a pitcher, the mound where he once stood so supremely confident became a place of struggle. In later years, Score disliked talking about the injury and the hand he was dealt, feeling that too much was made of it.

Score gave up on pitching and in 1964, began broadcasting television games for the Cleveland Indians and in 1968, slid behind the radio microphone and stayed. For the next 30 years, during some of the Indians' worst years as a franchise, he was a steady, reassuring constant. During times of 100-loss seasons, financial woes that threatened to take the team elsewhere, and games when it seemed the pigeons in Municipal Stadium's rafters outnumbered the fans in the stands, Score's low-key, comfortable voice was always there. His understated broadcasting style complemented that of his more up-tempo play-by-play partners. He was more like a favorite uncle visiting on the front porch on a warm summer's eve.

And Herb Score could make a mistake or two, sometimes mispronouncing a player's name, or forgetting what city he was in on a road trip. He would just chuckle and correct himself. But that was Herb. It just made him more human. More Herb. He stayed through all the bad years, and there were some truly awful ones until finally, good times came to Cleveland baseball. The team moved to a new stadium in 1994, followed by division titles, pennants, hundreds of consecutive sellout crowds, and World Series appearances in 1995 and 1997. After the latter, he switched off his microphone for the last time, perhaps knowing his work was done and he wasn't needed anymore.

Retirement years were unkind to this kind man. Score was terribly injured in an 1998 auto accident, made a slow recovery, followed by other health issues. His later years found him confined to a wheelchair, his familiar voice reduced to a whisper, his health ebbing. Cleveland's shoulders sagged and its eyes dampened when he passed in 2008. There he is remembered. There he is missed.

Entering the game for the NL in the bottom of the fourth inning and taking over the mound was pitcher Johnny Antonelli. He was quite the "bonus baby" when he signed with the Boston Braves in 1948 for the-then unheard of sum of $65,000. He wasn't used much the first couple of years, then served in Korea and returned to the Braves in 1953, who then lost interest in their once prized youngster and traded him to the New York Giants. The change in scenery turned out to be the tonic; he had an outstanding year in 1954, winning 21 games leading the NL in ERA, and helping lead the Giants to both a pennant and World Series. He would make four more All Star teams before the decade was over.

Also entering the game for the NL was New York Giant Willie Mays taking Jackie Robinson's spot in the outfield and playing in his first of what would be 24 All Star games. One of the most shopworn clichés in sports over the years has been, "He can do it all." Except, Willie really could. Everything. And not only superbly but with exuberance and elegance. The year 1954 was his first full year in the majors after playing much of the 1951 season, followed by 2 years in the Army. He responded by leading the NL in batting average, winning the Most Valuable Player award, and leading the Giants to the pennant and World Series against the heavily favored Cleveland Indians who had piled up a record 111 wins in rolling over the rest of the American League.

In game one of the Series with game tied in the eighth inning and two runners on, Cleveland's Vic Wertz smashed a line drive deep into the canyon that was the Polo Grounds centerfield, a sure triple or inside-the-park home run. Willie Mays, however, had a different idea. He sprinted with his back square to home plate, and without turning his head, reached out his glove and caught the ball in full stride as it whizzed over him. He whirled and flung the ball back to the infield as he fell down while disbelieving Indian base runners scrambled back to their bases. The catch is still considered to be the greatest in World Series history. "I had it all the way," he joked after the game. The Giants escaped the inning with the game still tied and went on to win that game in extra innings and stun the Indians in the series with a 4–0 sweep.

But two-and-a-half months before that catch, Mays was relaxing in a Cleveland hotel room with All Star teammate Roy Campanella, where the reticent Mays reluctantly agreed to an interview. A music lover, the sounds of jazz filled the room from a portable record player he lugged on road trips with him. He told a *Cleveland Press* reporter that he was ready for the game—that he had played in Cleveland "many times"— thus was familiar with the outfield he'd be patrolling.

Mays, however, was thinking of the Indians old home, League Park, and its very quirky outfield distances where he had played as a teenager in the Negro Leagues, unaware of the existence of Municipal Stadium. Campanella roared with laughter. "Not that park, he said, "This is the big stadium down by the lake. The biggest baseball park in the country. Why you could put League Park inside the stadium." Ever the ball player, Mays immediately asked about its outfield dimensions.

Later, eligible bachelor Mays was asked about his love life. "No time for girls," he said, "I've got to make a lot of money before I think of getting married. Takes a lot of money to get married these days." Campanella needled him a bit more. "I'll give you one year Willie, just one year. Especially if you stay around New York all winter. One year, remember." Willie responded, "Not me. You know I can run pretty fast." Mays did get married about a year and a half later on Valentines Day, 1956.

Mays's entrance into the game now meant that all three of New York City's great center fielders were in the same game at the same time: Willie Mays of the Giants, Mickey Mantle of the Yankees, and Duke Snider of the Dodgers. New York was the center of the baseball universe then with at least one New York team in the World Series from 1949-to-1958. Arguments would rage among Big Apple baseball fans over which was the best one. Over time, however, Willie Mays's achievements and sheer longevity would outshine the others.

Mays would go on to be the greatest player in Giants history, playing for 21 years. However the City of New York would only be able to claim him for five of those years as the Giants moved west with the Dodgers after the 1957 season. The Giants' exodus did not generate anywhere near the angst that the leaving of their Brooklyn counterparts did. Attendance had been down, the club had not been profitable in recent years and the emotional bond the team had with New York's five boroughs paled with that of the Dodgers and the neighborhoods of Brooklyn. Regardless, the Giants left countless numbers of broken-hearted fans in their wake.

On September 29, 1957, 3 years to the day of Willie Mays's great World Series catch, the Giants Hank Sauer grounded out to shortstop in the bottom of the ninth inning, bringing an end to the game and to the season. Some in the stands charged the Polo Grounds field seeking souvenirs while others chanted, "Stay, Team Stay" and "We Want Willie." Neither was going to happen and the New York Baseball Giants, after 72 years, faded forever to black. The Dodgers also played their last game that day and, incredibly, New York City had lost two of its three baseball teams in almost the blink of an eye.

Jackie Robinson's day was now done. He would play in two more All Star games before calling it quits after the 1956 season, his hair already gray, the body that was so supremely athletic going on to betray him in his postplaying days. A nearly blind and diabetic Jackie would make his final public appearance October 14, 1972, in Cincinnati, throwing out the ceremonial first pitch in game two of the World Series. He said at the time how much he would like to see a black manager in the dugout someday.

If he could have hung on a few more years he would have seen Frank Robinson, no relation, take the field as player-manager for the Cleveland Indians on Opening Day 1975, in the same stadium where he was today. He died, however, just 10 days later of a heart attack at the age of 53. On April 15, 1997, the 50th anniversary of his major league debut, major league baseball honored him with ceremonies in all the ball parks and permanently retired #42, the number he wore on his back.

The man whose torch Jackie Robinson picked up and carried, Moses Fleetwood Walker, went on to own and edit a newspaper and in 1908, perhaps with words like Cap Anson's ringing in his ears, published a pamphlet in which he urged blacks to emigrate to Africa, that life in

America could offer them only "failure and disappointment." He did not live long enough to see Jackie Robinson forever shatter baseball's color barrier. Nor did he live long enough to see an intersection outside the new Mud Hens stadium in Toledo named Moses Fleetwood Walker Square with a bronze plaque at the main gate telling his story.

Pitcher Bob Lemon was due to bat for the American League in the bottom of the fourth inning, and Manager Casey Stengel needed a pinch hitter. The decision was rather easy. Waiting on the bench was Ted Williams, in the twilight of his career but arguably the best pure hitter to ever touch a major league bat. Thirteen years earlier, Ted Williams had his own decision to make. It was the last day of the 1941 season and his batting average stood at .39955 which was .400—statistically, the Holy Grail of hitting.

His Red Sox were playing a doubleheader that day and the Boston manager left it to him whether to play or not. The decision for Williams was rather easy as well. Not only was he supremely confident in his ability as a hitter, he felt that if he couldn't maintain his average all the way through, he didn't deserve it. He merely banged out six hits in eight at bats in the twinbill to raise his average to .406. No player has had an average that high since or is ever likely to, although Williams gave it a try, batting .388 16 years later at the age of 39.

Hitting was the uncomplicated thing in Williams's baseball life. Other areas weren't as uncluttered. His personality ran on the prickly side and he had a love–hate relationship with the Boston fans while with the media, it was more of a truce–hate. When angry with the hometown faithful for real or perceived misbehavior, Ted could not accept fans booing him or anyone else—he would spit toward the stands or make an obscene gesture. He not only carried bat on his shoulder, he carried a chip as well.

Williams's career statistics were impressive considering he lost a total of five seasons to military service, in World War II and in Korea. He was not happy about being called back to the latter, feeling he had already done his duty, but his skills as a pilot were needed.

Ted Williams had just returned from Korea in 1953 and was invited to the All Star game in Cincinnati by Casey Stengel to sit on the bench as a guest, according to columnist Joe Knack of the *Toledo Blade* who was in Cleveland to cover the 1954 game. "As Ted walked across the field, the fans gave him one of the greatest ovations we've ever heard. Ted waved a friendly hand to the crowd. He was touched. Tears filled the eyes of this hard-bitten loner and history was made. It was the first ovation not accompanied by boos we ever heard Williams get, and his friendly wave to the crowd was probably his first too. So one of the really greats of baseball had to have his hard shell cracked at an All Star game." (Excerpt taken with permission of *Toledo Blade*, July 13, 1954).

But if dealing with human beings was problematic for Williams, hitting a round ball with a round bat was not. Few players studied hitting the way he did, which was as much a science to him as a physical act. When he wasn't actually hitting, he loved to talk about hitting—he probably dreamed about hitting—and eventually, he wrote about hitting. His 1970 book, *The Science of Hitting*, remains a well-regarded tutorial today.

In the bottom of the fourth inning for the American League, Chico Carrasquel singled to left, Ted Williams struck out, and Minnie Minoso lined a shot to right center field, Willie Mays's barehanded grab and throw back to the infield keeping it a single while Carrasquel moved to third. Bobby Avila lifted a sacrifice fly to left to score Carrasquel and Mickey Mantle grounded to third to end the inning. Score: National League 5, American League 5 after four innings.

In Arkansas, Tuesday's *Hope Star* featured a page one photo of a 12-year-old horse named Prince with a very pronounced sway in his back. His owner, a local man, explained that the steed was born that way and was a good worker who liked to play and go for rides.

Also on page one was a chilling wire story from Jackson, Mississippi: "Mississippi May Abolish Public School." Racism and fear of change manifested themselves in a proposed amendment to the state constitution to allow the abolishment of public schools statewide by a two-thirds majority vote of the state legislature or on a local option basis in order maintain segregation. The move was in response to the decision handed down in May by the U.S. Supreme Court in the Brown v. Board of Education case. The ruling held that "separate educational facilities were inherently unequal," thus unconstitutional. The state's governor said he would call the legislature into special session in September to consider the amendment. In a news story that read more like an editorial; "The amendment is viewed as safeguard if Negroes try to force school integration. It could be held over their heads as a threat—cooperate or lose your public schools."

In Boston this All Star Tuesday, *The Boston Post*, once one of the most popular papers in New England, was fading, printing only 22 pages this date, but no less feisty. In a page one editorial, the Post ripped the liberal New Hampshire biweekly, *The Reporter*, for an opinion piece criticizing Republican Senator Styles Bridges of that state, referring to the paper's critique as the "Great Smear."

The editorial in question, "Senator Styles and His Far Flung Constituents," alleged that in his positions as chairman of the Senate Appropriations Committee and ranking majority member of the Armed Services Committee, Styles was in a unique position to provide that "readily negotiable Washington currency called influence." It was certainly not the first, or last time, that such a charge was made regarding a politician in Washington or anywhere else.

Rather than rebut the specific allegations, the *Post* compared the editorial philosophies of *The Reporter* toward the senator to that of the *Daily Worker*, then the paper of the Communist Party in the United States, and wondered if it was "pro-communist, misguided, ultra-liberal, left of left wing, or what have you." The editorial then went on to note the strong anticommunist sentiments of New Englanders in general and that, "more often than not" the neighbors of anyone even suspected of having communist sympathies were inclined to believe it, which seemed to have nothing to do with the matter at hand. Ironically the editor of *The Reporter*, Max Ascoli, an unapologetic liberal, would go on to be a hawk on the Vietnam War.

New Hampshire's powerful Styles Bridges was also President pro tem of the Senate at the time. He had recently had been linked to a chain of sordid political events that ended in tragedy, according to syndicated columnist Drew Pearson. Late in 1953, a message was delivered from fellow conservative Republican Senator Herman Welker of Idaho via a third party to Senator Lester Hunt, a Wyoming Democrat and bitter opponent of Senator Joseph McCarthy.

The message to Hunt was simple; he was to drop his reelection bid in 1954 or the arrest of his son for allegedly soliciting a Washington D.C. undercover officer posing as a male prostitute would become a public matter. Young Hunt had been arrested and charged with a misdemeanor the previous June but, as a first-time offender, prosecution was withheld as the issue had been referred to his family and his church for resolution. He was a student at a theological school and studying for the ministry.

The Republicans held 48 senate seats to the Democrats 47 with one independent going into 1954, and the popular Hunt was expected to keep his seat in November. After a period of soul-searching, he refused to withdraw from the race. According to what Hunt told Pearson and others, an inspector with the Washington vice squad, under direct pressure from Bridges and Wexler, moved the at-the-time moot matter involving his son on to trial. Hunt sat through the proceeding, looking like he "was almost dying before men's eyes," in the words of Pearson, and his son was convicted and fined.

Fearful that in the aftermath that his boy would be used as campaign fodder, and facing some health issues, he changed his mind and withdrew from his senate race. Days later on June 19, 1954, a despondent Lester Hunt walked into his senate office, a .22 caliber rifle concealed under his coat. He fired a bullet into his brain and died a few hours later on an operating table. The notes he left did not give a reason. One to his son, however, said that he wasn't to blame.

An outcry followed Hunt's death; he had confided in a number of people of the behind-the-scene events taking place the previous months and many were calling it a "blackmail suicide." In July, Bridges and Wexler produced an affidavit from the vice squad inspector stating that he hadn't been pressured by them. However, as a friendly biography of Bridges published in 2001 wondered, how a dated and forgotten misdemeanor arrest suddenly came to the fore, with tragic consequences, was never satisfactorily explained.

In sports, the historic rivalry between Boston and New York seeped through in a grumpy column by *Boston Post* sportswriter Gerry Hern, criticizing Yankees and American League Manager Casey Stengel for selecting Yankee pitcher Whitey Ford, whose record was seven and six going in, to start the game. "Picking Ford was a rock," wrote Hern, rock—a now somewhat dated term for blunder—"It was unfair to the other pitchers and unfair to the All-Star game."

Hern went on to refer to the sometimes linguistically-less-than-eloquent Stengel as having a native tongue of "swerbel-berble" and pointed out that he was "the most beaten manager in All-Star history." He mentioned that Stengel "wins every American League pennant" but did not mention his current streak of five consecutive World Series titles, then implied that the greater portion of credit for the Yankees' recent success should go to General Manager George Weiss. Ford went on to pitch three scoreless innings, giving up only a single and a walk to the National League's powerful lineup.

Also in sports, "Jimmy Piersall's delighted to be here and just hopes Stengel will give him at least a chance to display his fielding wares." On this day, Boston Red Sox outfielder Piersall was getting a chance to display his coaching wares as well with a guest column in the *Post* aimed at youngsters on getting the jump on the ball when playing the outfield. Piersall had recovered from his problems of a couple of years earlier and, as a major league ballplayer, was coming into his own. The same could not be said for *The Boston Post*, which once could boast of a million readers, and which rolled its presses for the last time in 1956.

Jimmy Piersall was playing in his first of two career All Star games and his selection as an All Star was another step in a remarkable if not heroic comeback from an "injury" that would have ended the career of a less determined player. Just under two years earlier, Piersall awoke in a hospital room, sun from a nearby window streaming across his face, and unable to move. He was in the "violent room" of Westborough State Hospital in Massachusetts, strapped tight to a bed, with no recollection of how he got there.

Piersall's hellish 1952 season began in spring training in Florida when the Red Sox tried to convert the rookie outfielder into a short-stop, a difficult task for any player, and one that greatly increased the anxiety level of an already highly strung young ballplayer. Jimmy Piersall made the club and came north to Boston where the hyperactive Jimmy became even more so—entertaining fans with various on-field antics.

Piersall mimicked other players, did calisthenics in the outfield, flexed his muscles like a weightlifter, bowed deeply toward the stands after making routine catches, and talked constantly—be it with the fans or in the dugout and locker room. He quickly became a fan favorite, not only in Boston but on the road, as his reputation as the new clown prince of baseball spread. However teammates, opposing players, and in particular umpires, whom he baited constantly, were taking a distinctly different view.

Piersall was having a good rookie year, playing both shortstop and in the outfield and hitting well, but his behavior continued to escalate and, after a couple of clubhouse fights with teammates was sent down to minor league Birmingham at the end of June which devastated him. He had spent the previous season at Birmingham and Red Sox man-agement hoped he might calm down away from the pressures of a major league environment. However, things got worse there, and in less than 3 weeks, he was thrown out of six games and suspended four times.

On one occasion Piersall heckled the umpires from the stands after being tossed from a game, while on another, stood behind his Bir-mingham manager who was arguing a call with the home plate umpire and imitated his every move. And in a classic performance, he pulled a water pistol from his pocket after he was called out on strikes, squirted off home plate and told the umpire, "Now maybe you can see it." As in Boston, the fans roared with laughter, unable to see the dark river running underneath.

Piersall twice flew back to Boston on days off and on his second trip, was convinced by his wife Mary and Red Sox President Joe Cronin to check into a private sanitarium which he did, albeit reluctantly. There the dam broke and he became violent and he was transferred to the state system where things went dark for a while.

Piersall came to in early August at the state hospital in Westborough. A series of shock treatments the hospital had given him had stilled the rage within, but also wiped out his memory of most of the events of that year. (Shock treatment, now known as Electroconvulsive Therapy (ECT), was widely used in the 1930s to the 1950s to control symptoms such as mania before the advent of modern medicines. One of the side effects was of ECT was amnesia. It is used very selectively today.)

With the help of a good psychiatrist and the support of family and friends, Piersall got better and he walked out of the hospital in September. The following season he was back with the Red Sox, as an outfielder only, and played in nearly every game and batted a respectable .272. In 1954, he was deeply honored when Casey Stengel selected him as a reserve for the All Star game in Cleveland; he had developed into an excellent fielder whose glovework had drawn comparisons with Joe DiMaggio. And in 1955 he wrote a book called *Fear Strikes Out*, telling the story of his plunge into mental illness and the climb back out—made into a movie in 1957. The book he wrote was remarkable for its courage and honesty—it was written at a time when mental illness was one of those subjects talked about in hushed tones—if at all.

Piersall would go on to play until 1967, picking up Gold Glove awards in 1958 and 1961 and although calmer, was still a clown and crowd favorite with occasional flashes of his former volatility. Fans still laughed at his antics and umpires still tossed him out of games. He played with Cleveland from 1959 to 1961 and left his mark—a relatively brief, Indians pictorial team history published a few years later devoted an entire page to him with the headline, "The Wild One."

In 1962 in one of the ultimate "hot dog" moments in baseball history, Piersall turned around and ran the bases backward on the occasion of hitting his 100th career home run. After his playing career, he stayed plugged into baseball in various ways including coaching and broadcasting. He did the color commentary on White Sox television broadcasts for 6 years, teaming with the legendary Harry Caray, before crossing town and beginning a long coaching career in the Cubs organization.

Fifth Inning

Entering the game for the American League in the top of the fifth inning was Washington Senators' pitcher Bob Porterfield. His was the first of two Senators' teams in the nation's capital, the first lasting from 1901 to 1960 when the American League expanded, sending that team to Minnesota to become the Twins and placing an expansion team in the District of Columbia. The second coming of the Senators lasted only 10 years when that franchise moved to Texas after the 1971 season to become the Rangers. Futility marked the Senators last 30 or so years in Washington, a city that became known as, "first in war, first in peace, and last in the American League."

Porterfield played for 5 teams in 8 years and was making his only All Star game appearance. His presence in the 1954 game was a bit odd considering he was having an average year, 9–7 at the time, and would lead American League pitchers for the year in the dubious category of hits allowed. He did have an excellent year in 1953, winning 22 games and, in the role of workhorse, lead the league with 24 complete games and 9 shutouts, All Star numbers to be sure—entire pitching staffs don't have 24 complete games in a year anymore. Perhaps his selection was a "make up" for 1953.

In the top of the fifth inning for the National League, Alvin Dark lined out to center, Duke Snider singled to right, and Stan Musial popped out to the shortstop. Big Klu, Ted Kluszewski flexed his great biceps and slammed a long home run to right-scoring Snider, and Ray Jablonski grounded out to third to end the inning. Score: National League 7, American League 5 in the middle of the fifth inning.

In the old money and grandly mansioned community of Newport, Rhode Island this All Star Tuesday, workers were putting the finishing touches on a temporary, music shell with cardboard panels at the historic, Newport Casino. Local scions Elaine and Louis Lorillard had an idea to stage an annual jazz festival, a bit of a scandalous idea to some as jazz was then associated with race and with boozy, smoke-filled late-night clubs with audiences and performers of questionable moral fortitude. But the country had never had a major jazz festival and the Lorillards were determined to celebrate this original American art form; they provided the all-important financial backing. Louis's great-grandfather Pierre had established the Lorillard Tobacco Company years before the American Revolution; one of the company's cigarette brands was Newport.

The following Saturday, a Greyhound Bus packed with musicians and instruments rolled in from New York City and jazz luminaries such as Ella Fitzgerald, Dizzy Gillespie, Stan Kenton, and Oscar Peterson filled the night air with sound and the Newport Jazz Festival was born. The next evening, the cardboard walls of the shell sagged inward under a pelting rain, and the cold, damp crowd sat entranced as the legendary Billie Holiday sang her blues.

The event was a success, even turned a small profit, and is considered to be the grandfather of American jazz festivals. It has survived name and location changes, the intrusion of rock and other music genres and the loss of sponsors. In more than five decades of existence, jazz has gained widespread acceptance and festivals celebrating it can now be found in communities all over the United States.

In the desert environs of Reno, Nevada, the warm weather was hardly newsworthy this Tuesday but the annual Governors Conference was taking place in Bolton Landing, New York. The *Reno Evening Gazette* featured a page one photo of Vice President Richard Nixon being welcomed to the gathering by New York Governor Thomas E. Dewey and his wife, the vice-president filling in for President Eisenhower who was unable to attend because of the death of his sister-in-law. Also in this day's *Gazette* was an ad featuring the Duke Ellington Orchestra, which was headlining at the Stateline Country Club and Casino in Lake Tahoe.

Fourteen years later on the occasion of his 70th birthday, Ellington was invited to the White House of then President Nixon to be presented the Medal of Freedom. When the president hung the medal around his neck, Ellington responded by kissing him four times, twice on each cheek. "Four kisses?" a somewhat surprised Nixon asked. Said Ellington, "One for each cheek, Mr. President."

It was at the Governors Conference the country was hearing about President Eisenhower's bold new road plan in any detail for the first time. He envisioned a modern, multi-lane, high-speed highway network that would link cities and states and provide not only an unprecedented automotive transportation system but, very importantly in his mind, an evacuation route from urban areas in the event of a nuclear attack and transportation routes for military vehicles.

An Army convoy crossed the country in 1919 from Washington D.C. to San Francisco via the Lincoln Highway. The convoy was designed to test the vehicles and show the public the equipment used in World War I. Eisenhower, then a lieutenant, had gone on the tour and had enjoyed himself, saying it was kind of like going on a long camping trip. But it was a revealing one in that he was able to witness first hand the relatively poor condition of the nation's hodge-podge highway system—there were no paved roads between Illinois and California—and the trip took 2 months, averaging about 6 miles per hour. He had been impressed with Germany's autobahn highway system while there during World War II and wanted such a system in the United States. However, he had to convince the governors of 48 states first.

"Ike's Road Plan Jars Governors" read the July 13 headline in *The Cleveland Press* which pretty much reflected headlines around the country. In a speech that "shocked some governors," Vice-President Nixon, pinch-hitting for the president, outlined the president's plan at the Governors Conference taking place in New York for what would one day become the Interstate Highway System. The governors were all for new roads but saw the federal oversight of highway building as another intrusion into states' rights. They preferred funding be turned over to the states and each conduct their own road-building program, creating the potential for 48 different programs built at 48 different rates of speed.

However Eisenhower knew that federal oversight was the only way to go and eventually prevailed. On June 29, 1956, he signed into law the National System of Interstate and Defense Highways and construction began on what would become the greatest highway system the world had seen. His original idea was for these new highways to be built through rural and lightly populated areas and to go around cities and not into them, not wanting to see money spent on the acquisition of expensive, urban land. However, in order to get unenthused congress-men from urban areas to go along, Eisenhower's congressional liaison, on the sly, slipped in an urban road aspect which was what sold the whole idea. Senators, and in particular, urban House representatives, drooled over the prospect of federal highway money and the jobs that came with them flowing into their districts.

Three years later on a trip to Camp David, the president was dis-mayed to see a freshly dug cleave in the land just outside of Washington D.C. that was to be the path of one of these new highways, and learned, for the first time, that many of these interstates would be either passing directly through cities or connecting with them via a spur. Costs aside, he found it ludicrous that people would soon be commuting on a daily basis, one person per car in most cases, into cities that would then have to provide parking for all these new cars. He even proposed a special tax on these new commuters, which didn't go anywhere, believing mass transportation should be the answer.

But the toothpaste was out of the tube and, nearing the end of his second term, there was nothing he could do. His interstate system was going to be an inter- and intra-city one as well and a darned expensive one at that. Eisenhower correctly foresaw commuter-choked urban freeways—Washington D.C.'s rush hour traffic is brutal—years before they actually occurred.

What Eisenhower and others did not, or could not, have not seen at the time was the far-ranging social and economic impacts the interstate highway system would have on the United States over the next 40 years. The law of unintended consequences holds that any major action will produce unanticipated results or consequences and the building of the interstates represents a case study of this.

Cities were sliced up by new concrete boundaries, suburbs grew explosively, railroads declined while the trucking industry thrived and office complexes, warehouses, truck terminals, shopping centers, factories and even schools were built where the interstate, logically, dictated they should be built—very near or right along side.

Cities and towns that interstates passed through or adjacent to grew while many of those "inland" from the new highways went into gradual decline. In larger cities, rush-hour traffic jams became a weekday feature with the accompanying air pollution from engine exhaust. And locally owned motels and restaurants on state and U.S. routes closed, to be replaced by ones owned by national chains on the new and exalted interstate.

But as the new concrete highways rolled across the land, Americans discovered a love affair with the automobile and of the freedom of hitting the open road and were seeing the country as they never had before. For example, with the building of I-75, one could drive from Detroit to Florida in less than two days, a tempting prospect when in the grip of a Great Lakes winter, and a journey that could take three times that on the old Dixie Highway that I-75 replaced. And a coast-to-coast drive similar to the one Eisenhower took in 1919 could be done in less than a week instead of 2 months.

For millions in the closing decades of the twentieth century, the red, white, and blue interstate sign represented not a costly, federal highway project inspired by the need to evacuate cities in the face of a thermonuclear confrontation between superpowers, but the road to treasured vacations or holidays with loved ones. Interstate highways quickly became an integral part of the national infrastructure more than anyone could have imagined and many Americans, particularly those in urban areas, use one virtually every day of their lives.

The urgent need for better roads in the country, and the politics connected with that, was in evidence this day on page one of *The Cincinnati Enquirer*: "Cincinnati-St. Louis Toll Road Is Proposed," read the headline. Seeking to run with the ball before the federal government got into the game, the governors of Ohio, Missouri, and three other states were suggesting a toll road be built and operated under state control, providing the feds turn over the 2 cent per gallon gasoline tax it was collecting. In the end, the interstate highway system was built under federal oversight and today Interstates 74 and 70 link the cities of Cincinnati and St. Louis—no toll needed.

In the handsome, northern resort town of Traverse City, Michigan, where cherry trees glow with millions of pounds of tart cherries every summer, the headline atop page one of the *Traverse City Record Eagle* read "State Alarmed by Shothole Fungus Here." Michigan produces about 75 percent of the country's tart cherry crop, the majority in the Traverse City region, so any appearance of a fungus was cause for apprehension.

Also on page one of the *Record Eagle*—"Polio Do's—Don't's,"—an article listing practical safeguards against polio that was spread through person-to-person contact. Despite the trial introduction of the Salk vaccine in the spring, the paralyzing disease that seemed to strike from nowhere was still a parent's nightmare in the summer of 1954; there were nearly 58,000 new cases of polio just 2 years earlier, the most reported ever. Polio could strike persons of any age but the majority were children and it was children that the disease treated the most cruelly.

Summer and early autumn were the peak times for its occurrence with its symptoms of fever, pain, and respiratory difficulties. Although the bulk of its victims survived polio, the resulting nerve damage left many with varying degrees of paralysis. Polio's painful and disabling legacy included withered limbs, heavy leg braces, wheelchairs, crutches and for those unable to breathe on their own, the coffin-like iron lung. But in the summer of 1954, there was real hope for a cure.

America's polio nightmare began in summer of 1916 with an outbreak in Brooklyn that eventually spread to 26 states. Polio, then called infantile paralysis, had been a relative rarity in the United States up until then and initially doctors and public health officials were baffled. Ignorance and fear ruled early on as reflected in articles in the July 26 *New York Times*. One, "Paralysis Figures Rise In Manhattan" listed the names and addresses of all the new cases (150) and deaths (38) reported in the city's Boroughs just the previous day, the majority in Brooklyn.

It also told the tragic story of a Staten Island man who loaded his sick, 5-year-old boy into his car, desperately trying to find someone who would treat him. The child died en route to an infirmary and the people there refused to receive his body into the morgue for fear of contamination. The man then drove around for hours before, finally, the city's Department of Health agreed to receive the young boy's body at a disinfecting station.

Another article, "72,000 Cats Killed In Paralysis Fear" told of New Yorkers turning out their pet cats and dogs in the mistaken belief they carried the disease. Since July 1, the local SPCA had collected, and put to death, 72,000 cats and 8,000 dogs despite statements by the health commissioner that cats did not carry the disease. By the time it ran its course, 27,000 people had come down with polio across the country in 1916 and 6,000 of them had died.

Future President Franklin D. Roosevelt contracted the disease in 1921 leaving him paralyzed from the waist down and leg braces and wheelchairs became a part of the rest of his life. He would go on to establish the National Foundation for Infantile Paralysis (NFIP) in 1938, the fundraising arm of which became the March of Dimes. Researchers worked intensely on a vaccine over the years and Dr. Jonas Salk achieved a breakthrough in the laboratory in 1952.

His vaccine received its first clinical trials when it was administered to 1.8 million U.S. and Canadian schoolchildren in the spring of 1954, kids dubbed "Polio Pioneers." Salk was not without his critics. Dr. Albert Sabin, who was working on his own vaccine, vehemently opposed its use. And noted radio broadcaster of the day, Walter Winchell, predicted the vaccine would be a failure and irresponsibly accused the NFIP of stockpiling thousands of "little white coffins" for all the deaths that would follow, which needlessly frightened already worried parents.

The 1954 trial was a success and in April, 1955, the Salk vaccine was pronounced to be safe for widespread use and vaccinations began nationally. There was a problem initially as more than 200 recipients of the Salk vaccine did develop the disease and 10 died. This was later traced to an improperly prepared batch of the drug. This was quickly corrected and polio in the United States began a trip to the history books. Ultimately, the vaccine developed by Dr. Sabin was more effective and easier to administer and the Sabin vaccine, introduced in 1961, became the preferred vaccination method as polio cases in the United States quickly fell to a handful per year.

On this All Star Tuesday, a *Cleveland Plain Dealer* article carried the headline, "French Plan For Evacuation Is Set." In the aftermath of World War II, France had attempted to reassert its colonial dominance over Viet Nam only to find that communist rebels, led by Ho Chi Minh had a very different plan. Years of fighting had culminated in a decisive French defeat at Dien Ben Phu in May, and now preparations were being made to quickly evacuate the 6,000 French civilians who remained in the provincial capitol of Hanoi should the situation reach a "crisis stage."

French troops were manning "last ditch defense lines" just south of the city, while negotiations were taking place in Geneva for a turnover of power and a partitioning of the country. France would soon leave Viet Nam disgraced and humiliated. History, when ignored, has an unfortunate way of repeating itself and 21 years later, the United States would make a similar, even more desperate retreat from the capitol city of Saigon in South Viet Nam as North Vietnamese forces were ready to storm the city.

In the radio listings for the day, Cleveland's WJW-AM was broadcasting a listening menu typical of the day, music and talk provided by local radio hosts with news at the top of the hour. In the 4:00 P.M. and again in the 11:15 P.M. time slot was the simple line entry "Moon Dog," a pseudonym for Alan Freed, a local DJ who would become known as the "father of rock and roll." Freed had been a top-rated radio host in Akron the late 1940s before leaving the station in a salary dispute. He ended up in Cleveland, hosting an afternoon movie show on one of the city's early television stations, his talent wilting on the vine.

He got back into radio, spinning classical music albums on WJW in 1951 when he met up with Leo Mintz, a local record store owner. Mintz owned a large shop near Cleveland's burgeoning, black, east side neighborhoods and was looking for exposure for rhythm and blues records, then the up-tempo music of African-American musicians, also known then as "race music."

Mintz had noticed an increase in interest in this music by young whites coming into his store and wanted to rent late-night time on Saturday night on WJW for Freed to play the R&B discs, a proposal the skeptical DJ eventually agreed to. (Rock and roll legend holds that Freed went to Mintz's store, saw numbers of white kids pawing through the R&B sections and saw a music revolution in its infancy and ran with it. More fable than fact—much of it driven by Freed himself.)

What Freed did bring to the table was an energy and drive when he first went on the air on a July night in 1951. In no time, the boyish-looking, clean-cut Freed forever left Bach and Beethoven behind and evolved into the on-air persona of "Moondog," who invited listeners into his "Moondog House." He howled like a dog, rang a cowbell, accentuated the music's beat by slamming his hand on a phone book and yelled into the microphone—Cleveland had heard nothing like it. His audience initially consisted of Cleveland's black community, but more and more, curious whites were tuning in and the line between the two audiences was starting to thin.

(At some point Freed began referring to his program as a rock and roll "party" or "session" and at some later point, perhaps not until after he left Cleveland, was the rock and roll tag applied to the actual music he was playing. The phrase "rock and roll" appeared frequently in the rhythm and blues records of the day as a euphemism for sex. At what exact time the phrase came to represent the multibillion dollar genre of music it does today is unclear, although Freed gets the credit, as he should.)

In March 1952, only 9 months into his gig, Freed organized a five-act concert of black performers, "The Moondog Coronation Ball," at the Cleveland Arena, a hockey hall that sat about 10,000. His initial fear that he wouldn't draw enough people to cover expenses proved to be unfounded when a mostly black crowd numbering nearly twice the arena's capacity overwhelmed the facility and a riot almost broke out. It is considered to have been the country's first ever rock concert and it ended early due to the crowd, but Freed reaped priceless publicity from the event and WJW increased his airtime. He was on to something big and the music industry was noticing.

In the summer of 1954, New York City and its big stage were calling and in September Freed left Cleveland and moved on, bringing rock and roll radio to the Big Apple over the airwaves of WINS for the princely annual salary annual of $75,000. In less than a year, Freed's popularity and WINS ratings were soaring. He also hosted live stage shows. Brooklyn's Paramount Theater was a favorite venue, bringing major black and white performers together.

By 1956, Freed was being heard locally via WINS programming, nationally by way of a syndicated show sponsored by Camel cigarettes called the "Camel Rock and Roll Party," and internationally, over the powerful AM and shortwave transmitters of Radio Luxembourg, broadcasting to continental Europe and the United Kingdom.

In addition, Freed appeared in two of what would be a total of five career rock-themed movies that year. The movies were dreadfully shallow in terms of plot, a minor consequence to hungry, young rock fans, but they provided visual images of some of the major acts of the day years before music videos made it to television. The film, *Rock, Rock, Rock* in which Freed was given control over the artists appearing, opened in December in more than 400 theaters nationally and nearly 80 in the New York metropolitan area.

Less than three months later, *Don't Knock the Rock*, debuted at the Paramount Theater on Broadway in combination with a stage show on Washington's Birthday in 1957. Young fans began lining up on Manhattan's cold streets at 1 A.M. to eventually pass under a marquee with "In Person Alan Freed" emblazoned across the top. By the following afternoon, 175 policemen were needed for crowd control and Alan Freed was very much on top. He was now living in a Connecticut mansion called Grey Cliffe and doing remote broadcasts from a studio there, something that left WINS management less than thrilled.

In the spring of 1958, Freed launched an extensive 6-week, "Big Beat" rock and roll tour across the Midwest and East Coast featuring Chuck Berry, Jerry Lee Lewis, and Buddy Holly as headliners. The tour rolled into Boston in early May where authorities were edgy after some trouble broke out after a couple of previous Freed productions. When the excited and dancing crowd spilled into the aisles of the Boston Arena, police threw on the house lights. After some back and forth between the police and Freed, he said into a microphone something along the lines of, "The police don't want you to have a good time." It was probably not the most judicious thing he ever said.

Within moments, mayhem broke out as rival gang members in the audience began fighting and the rest of the crowd fled the building and some violence continued outside. Exactly how much violence ensued or whether it could at all be attributed to Freed or his concert was secondary. In the media, the incident became a "rock and roll riot" and Freed himself was indicted by a grand jury a few days later for inciting the whole event.

The negative publicity led to the cancelation of several other concerts on the tour and contributed to the loss of his job at WINS. Freed had expected the station to help him fight the charges, which were later dropped, but instead it fired him. The Boston incident wasn't the sole reason; Freed, who had always been somewhat egotistical and abrasive, had become even more so with success and was wearing out his welcome at the station. By now, he was also becoming a lightning rod for social critics who saw the music he championed connected to youthful rebelliousness, sexuality, and the mixing of the races—a major taboo in the 1950s.

Freed was hired almost immediately by New York's WABC radio and, with an afternoon television show as well, things were good for a time. But his world began to unravel in November 1959, when he refused to sign an ABC management legal document stating he'd never taken money from record companies to play their records. He couldn't sign the document because to do so would have been perjury. He had taken money, and plenty of it, as had dozens of disc jockeys around the country in the 1950s. However the practice of "payola" was now going under a Congressional microscope. In later testimony, Freed freely admitted he took money, which he characterized as "gifts," but adamantly denied it affected his record-playing decisions.

Freed was fired immediately by WABC, an event that was front page news in all the New York papers, and his days as a big-time disc jockey and concert promoter were over. He increasingly sought refuge in alcohol and worked at radio stations in Los Angeles and then Miami, but was fired by both, the latter after less than 3 months near the end of 1962.

He spent his final few years drinking very heavily, dreaming of a return to big-time radio, unemployed and virtually unemployable, and being chased by the government for back taxes—in part, for not declaring his payola monies as income. He died penniless in 1965 in California at the age of 43 and was cremated, a forgotten and broken man who 10 years earlier had held New York City in his hand. Cirrhosis was the given cause of death although friends said he died of a broken heart.

In 1995, the Rock and Roll Hall of Fame and Museum rose on Cleveland's Lake Erie shore in what was once a Municipal Stadium parking lot, about a baseball's throw from the bleacher wall where the game was being played this day. Freed having been inducted into its initial class. In 2002, he was brought home and his ashes were interred in the Hall whose foundation he unwittingly laid when he began playing records on a Cleveland, late-night radio show 50 years before—a comet who'd shot across the rock and roll sky. Freed was not the first to air the music that would come to gather under the banner of rock and roll, but he was among the very first to recognize its enormous potential and brought it to a larger audience in a way no on else had.

Entering the game for the National League in the bottom of the fifth inning was St. Louis Cardinals second baseman Red Schoendienst, taking over that position for Granny Hamner, and playing in his seventh consecutive All Star game. That his first name reflected the Cardinals team color was appropriate considering he would have a seven-decade association with the organization, beginning in the 1940s and continuing into the new century. A skilled and fluid second sacker, an error by Red Schoendienst was a rare event indeed in his 18 years a player.

In 1956, Schoendienst set a National League Record for fielding percentage that stood for 30 years. He missed virtually the entire 1959 season due to tuberculosis, his comeback from which drew national attention. In 1965, he became the Cardinals manager, a spot he held for 12 years—a lengthy tenure—and led the team to the 1967 pennant and World Series victory over the Boston Red Sox, and another pennant in 1968. One of the most popular players in team history, the Cardinals have honored him by both retiring his number and erecting a statue of him outside their stadium.

Also coming in for the National League was Randy "Handsome Ransom" Jackson of the Chicago Cubs, taking over at third base for Ray Jablonski. A football player in college, Jackson played halfback in consecutive Cotton Bowl games, unusual because it was for two different teams, Texas Christian University and the University of Texas in 1945 and 1946, respectively. And this was after he initially started at the University of Arkansas. He had been forced to transfer from college to college as WWII wound down and the officer training programs he was enrolled in closed. He made consecutive All Star games in 1954 and

1955 and then was acquired by the Brooklyn Dodgers the following year in a major trade to take over for an aging Jackie Robinson at third base who was nearing retirement. Those plans came to an end when he seriously hurt his knee in 1957 and never played regularly again.

In the bottom of the fifth inning, Yogi Berra singled to left and Al (what sore finger?) Rosen blasted a 400-foot home run deep into the lower left field seats for his second homer of the game, his five RBI tying Ted Williams's record set in the 1946 All Star game. Pitcher Johnny Antonelli settled down after that as Ray Boone grounded out to third, Bob Porterfield flew out to left, and Chico Carrasquel struck out. Score: National League 7, American League 7 after five innings.

On this All Star Tuesday, water woes were featured in all three Cleveland newspapers as the hot, dry weather was not only parching the ground but straining the local supply. In particular, the newer, more distant suburbs were using the precious aqua about as fast as the Cleveland Water Department could pump it out to them. In Cleveland and in the rest of the country, an exodus was underway as millions were packing up and leaving forever the city where they had grown up.

In what had recently been a corn or wheat field, they found new and affordable homes, green space, clean air, good schools and low crime rates. Yes, in many case the lots were treeless and the tract homes looked remarkably similar to the one next door, or across the street, or in back or on the next block. For many now there was also a long commute to work with a lost connection to friends and family in the old neighborhood and their new communities lacked any sort of roots, story, or history.

But they did feature a degree of social homogeneity, a place where the neighbors tended to be couples of similar age and interests and a new suburban culture evolved where backyard barbeques, bowling leagues, and cocktail parties became the norm. Here, also, is where the baby boom boomed and suburban life became synonymous with family life. Kids could now play in their own yard instead of the street out front where Mom and Dad, growing up in the city, often played.

The modern suburb had its genesis in the mind of William Levitt who built housing for workers, simple four-room units on a slab, at the huge naval base in Norfolk, VA, during World War II. He envisioned that millions of GIs coming home after the war would soon want a home of their own. In 1947, he began building Levittown in a Long Island potato field, 30 miles from New York City, using assembled or partly assembled components as much as possible and achieving an assembly line-like efficiency. Despite reaching a peak production of 30 homes a day by the summer of 1948, he could not build them fast enough as house-hungry veterans and others snapped them up.

A similar scene repeated itself in dozens of other American cities including Cleveland, where a sleepy burgh named Parma, exploded from a population of fewer than 20,000 in 1950 to more than 110,000 by 1980. Over time, the Levittowns and Parmas of the country came to be viewed in somewhat derogatory terms. The 1967 Monkees' hit song, *Pleasant Valley Sunday*, lamented this, painting a scene of tedious suburban sameness of rows of identical houses with charcoal grills smoking and materialism abounding. Parma, with its generally blue collar, Eastern European population, even became the butt of jokes, led by local TV movie hosts who teased residents for putting plastic pink flamingoes in their yards.

But what these places did was allow young couples of moderate and even modest means to own a home of their own and the patch of ground around it. Here they lived and loved, raised a family, celebrated birthdays and anniversaries, retired, played with their grandchildren and finished their days. It was the post World War II American Dream, both perfect and imperfect.

Plastered across the top of page one in the *San Francisco Chronicle* this day was the headline, "New Raft Mercy Mission." Five men whose thoughts most definitely were not on the All Star game this day were aboard a large raft named Lehi, bobbing somewhere in the Pacific Ocean off the California coast. Led by an adventurer and a dreamer named DeVere Baker, a Mormon who believed it possible to drift from California to Hawaii, it had been in the ocean 4 days. Caught in a coastal current that dragged it well off course, the craft was also plagued by rough weather, leaks, and a radio operator who had become both physically ill and thoroughly sick of the journey and was sending continuous and frantic distress calls to anyone who would listen: "Get somebody out here while I'm still alive," went one.

The drama of a raft and crew in peril was page-one-news in many newspapers, particularly on the west coast. The crew was rescued a couple of days later in 15-foot seas by a banana boat. Baker asked the Coast Guard to tow the raft, which was loaded with expensive equipment. The Guard declined and, seeing it as a navigational hazard, instead sent it to the bottom of the ocean with a few well-aimed shells. Baker and the Coast Guard would go on to have a less than cordial relationship.

Baker was not about to give up. He'd planned his voyage as both a statement against war and to prove, as suggested in the Book of Mormon, that tribal people could have sailed in rafts from the Middle East to America's West Coast 600 years before the time of Christ. In the next few years he gave speeches and raised funds and there came a Lehi II then a Lehi III, neither of which fared much better than the original.

Finally in 1958, Baker, with a crew of three and a dog named Tangoroa aboard the Lehi IV, made it all the way to Hawaii in 69 days. As they neared the islands a Coast Guard cutter pulled alongside and boomed a message of acknowledgement over its public address system; "Congratulations Captain Baker, you have proved your point." Baker basked in celebrity status as news of the voyage spread worldwide. His planned future endeavors, such as a raft trip from the Red Sea to America and even one around the world, ran aground due to health problems. In 1980 he ran a short-lived campaign for president, traveling in a Greyhound bus, and promising to appoint a secretary of peace if elected. He died in 1990.

In news more local, San Francisco's Board of Supervisors was considering a law to ban "action sales" on the city's popular Market Street. The street was becoming a mecca for scam artists selling, watches that didn't run, junk jewelry, appliances that broke down in a few weeks, and guarantees that guaranteed nothing. The victims were mostly servicemen and tourists.

And in news of entertainment, "Lili St. Cyr Wows 'Em In Oakland Burlesque." Ms. St. Cyr, originally Willis Marie Van Schaack of Minneapolis, Minnesota, had dreams of being a ballet and chorus line dancer before she discovered there was a heck of a lot more money in taking her clothes off. She was presenting her Northern California premiere of her latest act in Oakland where she disrobed on stage and took a bubble bath; the *Chronicle* sent a reporter across San Francisco Bay to cover it.

St. Cyr had been arrested several years earlier and charged with indecent exposure when she performed a version of the routine in a Hollywood, California, spa. She was found not guilty, however, when the judge instructed the jury to determine if any of her audience, consisting of whistling, cheering men, were "annoyed" by her act. Apparently none were, as was no one at her standing- room only Oakland show.

Thanksgiving sales had been slow in 1953 for the food company, C.A. Swanson & Sons of Omaha, Nebraska, leaving them with a large supply of unsold turkey. Now what they needed was a demand. And they created that demand, more than they ever dreamed, by coming up with a frozen dinner with an image of a television on the package—the TV dinner. The first Swanson TV dinner was a replica Thanksgiving meal—turkey, cornbread dressing and gravy, sweet potatoes, and buttered peas selling for 98 cents.

Something about having an already cooked supper come in a neat, three-compartment tray that could be heated and served in the very packaging that it came in caught hold of the American imagination. And that neat little tray could be eaten off a lap tray or a small table while watching the new god of the household—the television. The company hoped to sell around 5,000 of them in 1954 but instead sold millions. (The author had a childhood fascination with these dinners, one that went unrealized for the most part, as his parents considered them to be frivolous and a bit pricey in a family of nine with one income.)

On this All Star Tuesday, a one-sentence story in *The Plain Dealer* told that 16 legislators from Japan on a Soviet Union visit went to Leningrad for a short stay before returning to Moscow, an inconsequential item. What is interesting is the headline over the story, "Japs In Leningrad." The use of the world Japs to refer to anyone Japanese was common during World War II before being exiled from general usage in the years that followed. It would be unimaginable for any media organization to use the reference today.

Sixth Inning

Coming into the game in the top of the sixth inning for the National League was Pittsburgh Pirates' outfielder Frank Thomas, playing in his first of three All Star games. Thomas, at this point in his life, could have been referred to as Father Thomas as he studied for the Catholic priesthood for several years before pursuing a professional baseball career. Instead, because of his sizable stature, he was anointed by his peers as "The Big Donkey," sports nicknames sometimes running on the juvenile side and this case being no exception. He played for seven teams over a 16-year career, his best years being with the Pirates from 1951-to-1958; in his last year there he was featured on the cover of *Sports Illustrated* magazine.

In the top of the sixth inning, Bob Porterfield remained on the mound for the American League and Willie Mays flew out to deep left field; Roy Campanella singled to right. Frank Thomas, pinch hitting for pitcher Johnny Antonelli, took a called third strike, the big donkey, and Red Schoendienst flew out to left. Score: National League 7, American League 7 in the middle of the sixth inning.

A story in *The Cleveland Press* this All Star Tuesday, "South Euclid Passes Curfew Law to Cope With Gangs of Rowdies," reflected a disturbing post World War II trend in America—in a time of rising prosperity, juveniles were increasingly being drawn to criminal activity. South Euclid, a solidly middle class Cleveland suburb, had passed emergency legislation mandating curfews for those aged under 18 with fines for their parents if noncompliant.

The previous weekend, New York City had been shocked when three Brooklyn teenagers, aged 15, 16, and 17 and described by their families as "good boys," savagely beat a 40-year-old father of four to death in what authorities described as a "thrill kill." As early as 1953, FBI statistics indicated a noticeable rise in juvenile crime. Theories at the time ranged from the plausible, poor home life, to the absurd—too much comic book reading.

Also in New York this day, a major Manhattan real estate announcement, corrupt New Jersey politics and an act of now antiquated honor were on page one of the *New York Herald Tribune*. Seagrams Distillers Corporation, then a Canadian liquors and spirits giant, announced plans to build a 34-story "House of Seagram" on Park Avenue to consolidate its U.S. operations. The structure, which topped out at 38 stories and is now known as the Seagram Building was completed in 1958 and designed by famed German architect Ludwig Mies van der Rohe whose belief that "less is more" was reflected in his work.

He used only 40 percent of allowable space in order that an open, granite plaza rolled from the building to the street, which proved to be so popular that New York City rewrote its zoning language in 1961 to encourage future construction projects to do the same. The House of Seagram became the inspiration for corporate office towers across the country and is considered to be an outstanding example of the International Style today.

Across the Hudson River in New Jersey, former Jersey City Mayor Frank Hague got into a shoving match the previous day with a sheriff's deputy who had served him a subpoena. Hague was being sued by Jersey City for extorting millions of dollars from city employees during his reign. He had flown in from Paris for the funeral of his nephew and was particularly offended by the timing of the matter, which took place in front of the funeral home. He yelled to the crowd in front, "Imagine an outfit like that serving a summons at this kind of service." In recent years he had stayed away from New Jersey, dividing his time between homes in Florida and on Park Avenue in Manhattan. And Local officials had been trying to serve the subpoena for months.

Frank Hague was a "boss mayor" if America ever saw one. He rose from the Irish slums of Jersey City to the mayor's office in 1917 and ruled almost without challenge for 30 years. Tough, shrewd, he knew how to get to the top and how to stay there. He once explained to *Collier's* magazine, "Politics is business. That's what the reformers don't get. They think it's sort of a revival meeting with nothing to do but nominate some bird who makes a lot of speeches about clean government, and then sit back and wait for the voters to hit the sawdust trail. That's a laugh. You got to have organization, and not just for a few weeks before the election but year 'round. Understand? What's more, an organization that reaches into every home in every block, so that the district worker knows every man, woman, and even children like he knows his own family. Get me?"

Hague presided over a finely-tuned Democratic Party political machine that was staffed, and financed, by a small army of city and county employees he had swelled payrolls with, who in return, kicked backed a percentage of their salaries. In 1932, the city listed two full-time "cuspidor cleaners" while the county could boast of a "foreman of vacuum cleaners." Other forms of municipal graft, cash only, could be paid directly through a special lap drawer in the mayor's desk that when pushed, opened outward toward the person sitting in front. The desk is still displayed in Jersey City's City Hall. Though his mayoral salary never exceeded $8,500 annually, his personal worth was estimated to have reached as high as $10,000,000.

Hague railed against communism and lumped labor unions into this category after initially being friendly toward them, yet practiced a form of municipal socialism in which he granted various favors and services to individuals at taxpayers' expense. This culminated in the building of Jersey City Medical Center, a 10-building complex with a

23-story surgery building that provided top-notch, and virtually free, medical care to city residents at considerable public expense.

In its large maternity center, named for the mayor's mother, thousands of Jersey City babies were literally born into his machine. The hospital was his pride and joy, he maintained an office there, and could frequently be seen strolling the halls, chatting with patients, wishing them well and reminding them who was responsible for the fine care they were receiving. Hague's motivation was not entirely selfish; he never forgot his impoverished roots. And both his parents suffered from poor health and could not afford adequate medical care. However, he was acutely aware of the political advantages as well. Who could vote against a mayor who gave you good medical care at little or no cost?

In 1947 he was in his seventies, growing more aloof, and spending much of his time in Florida. He resigned and turned his office over to his nephew who ran the machine until he was defeated in 1949. It was the funeral of this nephew he was attending in 1954 when he was served with the subpoena. Like the other investigative efforts aimed at him, this one went nowhere as the lawsuit against him was dismissed.

Hague died on New Years Day, 1956, and as and his 700-pound, hammered copper casket was lugged out of the same Jersey City funeral home, a voice called "Hats, men" to the crowd of several hundred onlookers gathered outside. Only four were observed to actually lift their hats in tribute. Frank Hague, who once famously declared, "I am the law," went to his burial in a fine, marble mausoleum with his name chiseled across the top, with the majority of his onetime former constituents realizing how lawless he actually was.

Also on the front page this day's *Herald Tribune* was a story of the sinking of a Panamanian freighter in the Indian Ocean. The ship had struck a reef 200 miles from Bombay and managed to stay afloat for 12 hours, which gave a British tanker and an Indian coastal ship responding to the scene adequate time to rescue the 34 crew members and 8 officers. The ship's captain, a New Zealander named C. H. Turner, ignored the frantic signals of his crew and rescuers and stayed with his ship until it slipped beneath the waves. Maritime tradition holds that a captain is duty bound to ensure the safe transfer of passengers and crew from his sinking ship, then is obligated to save himself. Why Captain Turner stayed with his doomed vessel, or what his final thoughts were, will never be known.

On an inside page was a note that a French actress named Denise Darcel, who once took a wild flight, was going to sing the French national anthem the next day in a musical celebration of Bastille Day at City College of New York. Darcel was a stunning young woman living in Paris during World War II who worked by day as a store clerk and by night in a secret factory making ammunition for the French Underground. When the Pacific theater of war ended on August 15, 1945, with Japan's surrender, thousands poured into the streets of Paris to celebrate.

As the story goes, Darcel, and her U.S. Army Air Corps pilot boyfriend, got into his small, two-seater spotter plane with champagne in their bellies and more in tow, and flew to Paris to celebrate. A skilled aviator, he flew under several bridges on the Seine River then spotted the Eiffel Tower. After checking it for guy wires and other obstructions, he flew under the great tower itself to the utter astonishment of those below. The next day, a London newspaper carried a story of the antics of a crazy American pilot who could not be identified but who had a female passenger along.

Darcel worked as a cabaret singer in Paris after the war then came to the United States to pursue a film career, the highlight of which was starring opposite Gary Cooper sand Burt Lancaster in the 1954 film *Vera Cruz*, a Western.

The *Herald Tribune* had sent two sportswriters to Cleveland to cover the game. One, a young reporter named Roger Kahn, was drooling over the prospect of the Giants' Willie Mays, the Cardinals' Stan Musial and the Dodgers' Duke Snider playing together in the same National League outfield: "It is possible to dream of a better outfield than Musial, Mays and Snider but it would take a rather searching dream. The young Babe (Mays) has hit thirty-one homers, Musial has hit like Musial and Snider has hit like Musial, too. Probably the best way to dream up a better outfield is to start the dream with a little hashish."

Brooklyn-born Kahn, who would go on to be one of the great baseball writers ever, was the Dodgers beat writer for the *Herald Tribune* in 1952 and 1953. He traveled with the team he grew up loving, not that many years removed from boyhood trolley rides to games with his father, Gordon Kahn. Both seasons brought thrilling pennants home to Brooklyn but both ended with crushing World Series losses to the Yankees and days after the 1953 loss, Gordon Kahn collapsed and died on a Brooklyn sidewalk. Roger Kahn was gone from the paper by 1955 and, as a spectator, watched as the Dodgers finally broke through the glass ceiling to bring home the team's and the Borough of Brooklyn's only World Series title. Two years after that, the Dodgers themselves were gone.

Around a decade later, Kahn began tracking down some of the players he covered during what was Brooklyn's golden, albeit final, chapter in baseball. What he found were men who once were of uncommon accomplishment now living in the realm of the common and approaching middle age, with life's many and varied triumphs, realities and tragedies. He then wove a wistful and evocative narrative of his coming of age in Brooklyn, his love of the Dodgers and the baseball bond he shared with his father, his days of traveling with the team and of the players he came to know, and of the ultimate and inevitable effects of the passage of time on them. From a line in a Dylan Thomas poem—"I see the boys of summer in their ruin"—came the title of his bestselling 1972 book, *The Boys of Summer*. ("I See the Boys of Summer," by Dylan Thomas, ©1939 by New Directions Publishing Corp., reprinted by permission).

But Roger Kahn knew none of this on this day as he was covering the upcoming All Star game with the excitement of a fan. He wrapped up his day-before-the game piece with this observation: "Tacked to the press room bulletin board was a somber sign. 'Attention All Writers, you are cordially invited to drop your expense account money at Thistle Downs race track. Your baseball writer's card will admit you. (Aside to auditor: We know they're kidding, don't we?'")

Also in the sports pages of the *Herald Tribune* this day was a note about a player who would never appear in an All Star game but would someday be elected to the Hall of Fame anyway. The Dodgers announced that they'd released a young outfielder by the name of Dick Williams outright to their minor league affiliate, the St. Paul Saints. The word "outright" usually means the player does not figure into the team's plans anytime soon, if ever.

Williams went on to play for a number of teams but would go on to make his mark as a manager. In 1967, the disciplinarian Williams drove the Boston Red Sox, who were coming off eight consecutive losing seasons, to the World Series where they were edged in seven games by the St. Louis Cardinals. That year in Boston became known as "The Impossible Dream" and Williams was named Manager of the Year by the Sporting News. And in 1972 and 1973, he led the Oakland A's to consecutive World Series titles. He was rewarded with enshrinement in the Hall of Fame in 2008.

If the boys of summer were in decline, so was the *New York Herald Tribune*. Born in 1924 when the *New York Tribune* acquired the *New York Herald*, by the end of that decade it was thriving under the leadership of legendary city editor Stanley Walker. The stereotypes of the position at the time—that of a loud, profane, desk pounding, ink-stained tyrant—did not apply to him.

He addressed reporters as "Mister," and believed that if the *Herald-Tribune* could not compete directly with the *New York Times* in sheer resources it could, on a consistent basis, turn out better written and more colorful copy. He nurtured his reporters in the art of writing, and the *Herald-Tribune* became known as the "newspapermen's newspaper" and was a magnet for talent. Combined with the already striking typography and design brought from the *Tribune*, it was considered to be one of the finest papers in the country.

In 1935, Walker moved on and that same year, a sensational murder trial was the backdrop for an episode in the intense competition between papers to "scoop" as newspapers were still the source of breaking news. Tension ran thick in the *Herald Tribune* newsroom in the dark evening of February 13. The jury in the Bruno Richard Hauptmann case, accused of kidnapping and murdering Charles Lindbergh's baby in what was called the crime of the century, had been deliberating all day and the paper was nearing its 11 P.M. time for its first edition to roll out the door. The nation, and for that matter the world, awaited the verdict and the paper had three possible outcomes already set in type and ready to print; not guilty, guilty with life imprisonment, and guilty with the death penalty.

In Flemington, New Jersey, where the trial was being held, the courthouse was cloaked in secrecy to prevent word from getting out prematurely. The Associated Press, equally competitive, had spies in place including one in the courthouse attic and almost 15 minutes before the verdict was formally announced, flashed the words—guilty with life in prison.

At the *New York Times*, the presses thundered into action but at the *Herald Tribune*, night city editor Lessing Engel chomped furiously on his cigar. Something was wrong. He couldn't understand why there was no death penalty, considering the magnitude of the crime. He wanted corroboration and agonizing minutes passed as word reached the newsroom that the *Times* delivery trucks were already hitting the streets. Then a flash from United Press, guilty with the death penalty, and still Engel wanted more. Finally the *Herald-Tribune's* reporter in Flemington got through and confirmed that indeed the electric chair awaited Hauptmann. The paper went with the right story while the *Times* rushed trucks back out to chase down the errant copies that were already being hawked on newsstands on the streets of New York.

It was still the "golden age of newspapers" although the waves of radio, and the immediacy they could bring, were already piercing the sky in increasing numbers. A few years later Edward R. Murrow electrified the country with his live reports from London for CBS radio during the Blitz, Germany's 9-month sustained bombing campaign of England from 1939 through 1940. Murrow's trademark opening, "This is London," had millions of Americans gathered around their living room sets. By 1942, New York City had 13 radio stations on the air and the days of print as the sole bringer of the news were in the past.

Television mushroomed in the 1950s; 1954 was the first year it became the country's number one advertising medium, which hemorrhaged revenue from newspapers; and it was clear that the field of newspapers would be significantly thinned in the coming years. In 1962 the struggling *Herald-Tribune*, brought famed writer Tom Wolfe aboard as a reporter and features writer but 4 years later, losing money and plagued by labor troubles, it rolled its presses for the last time—a light extinguished. Its name lives on in its European edition, *The International Herald Tribune*, which circulates in around 180 countries and is owned and operated by the *New York Times*.

Coming into the game for the National League in the bottom of the sixth inning was Milwaukee Braves pitcher Warren Spahn playing in his seventh of what would be 14 All Star games, a twentieth-century record for pitchers. He also owns the record for most career wins by a left-hander, an amazing 363. He was a Brave in every sense of the word, pitching for that franchise for 20 years, first in Boston and later in Milwaukee. A cerebral pitcher, he preferred to outthink, rather than overpower, a hitter.

In 1948, due to a combination of scheduled pitching starts, double headers, team days off, and rainouts, Spahn and fellow pitcher Johnny Sain managed to start, and win, an unheard of 8 games in just a 12-day period. This led a Boston scribe to compose a poem lauding the two, which eventually was condensed to "Spahn and Sain and Pray for Rain." The ditty has found a niche in baseball lore. Spahn and his teammate's efforts paid off as Boston won the National League pennant that year, its first since 1914 and last in Boston, before going on to lose to the Cleveland Indians in the World Series.

Also coming into the game for the NL was New York Giants pitcher Marv Grissom, making his NL All Star game appearance. He made his major league debut for the Giants in 1946, then bounced around in the minors and with several other major league teams before coming back to the Giants in 1953. He had his best year in 1954 when the Giants won both the pennant and World Series. While star and high-profile players get the lion's share of the credit when a team wins a title, just as important are players like Marv Grissom having that one good year when it's really needed. After his playing career, he was a major league pitching coach for 15 years for several different teams.

In the bottom of the sixth inning with Warren Spahn pitching, Ted Williams walked on four pitches and Minnie Minoso singled to right, Williams going to third on the hit and run. Bobby Avila singled to left, scoring Williams while Minoso motored around second and headed for third where Stan Musial's throw nailed him at the bag, Avila taking second. Mickey Mantle beat out an infield single to deep short, Yogi Berra popped to second, and Al Rosen, with a tremendous ovation accompanying him to the plate, slapped an infield single off the third basemen's shoulder to load the bases. Marv Grissom came in to pitch and Ray Boone to fly out to center to end the inning. Score: American League 8, National League 7, after 6 innings. If they weren't already, the fans in the stands in Cleveland as well as in the country's television and radio audiences were beginning to sense they were witnessing history.

Across the Atlantic ocean on this All Star Tuesday in England—America's largest ally—baseball was not on the mind of the British but nuclear weapons were. In March, the United States had detonated a hydrogen bomb on the Bikini Atoll in the Pacific Ocean. Observers were stunned at the massive mushroom cloud; it turned out to be about 1,000 times more powerful than the atom bombs dropped on Japan during World War II, which was much more than its designers expected. It blasted a crater 250 feet deep and over a mile wide in solid rock and spread radioactive fallout on residents of three other islands and on a Japanese fishing boat nearly 80 miles away, creating an international incident. An uncertain world had become a little more uncertain.

According to an editorial in *The* (London) *Times*, British Prime Minister Winston Churchill was troubled not only by the power of the new weapon but by the lack of information-sharing with

Britain—which went against the usual practice between the allies. Churchill had recently returned from Washington where he had traveled specifically to discuss thermonuclear matters. "I was deeply concerned at the lack of information we possessed," he told the British Parliament on Monday.

On his departure for Washington, there was concern in Britain that his reception there might be a chilly or even hostile one. "The contrary proved to be true," he said. "I have never had a more agreeable or fruitful visit than on this occasion and I never had the feeling of general good will more strongly borne in upon me." The Parliament ministers cheered.

An adjacent letter to the editor, signed by 11 residents of Oxford, called on the British government to declare that it would not launch nuclear weapons, including the hydrogen bomb, on a first-strike basis or allow any other country to do so, from military installations in any of its territories. President Eisenhower had made such a declaration earlier in the year.

And another editorial updated the rebuilding progress in seven English cities bombed by the Germans during World War II, 9 years after war's end. There were varying degrees of progress among the cities in reconstructing both residential areas and commercial districts, governed by such factors as availability of labor. It was estimated that the city with the least advancement, Canterbury, would need another 20 years to complete the job.

America had no experience of being bombed by a foreign power. To prepare the country for the possibility of such an event, President Harry Truman had created the Federal Civil Defense Administration (FCDA) in 1951, which used posters and other materials to educate the public. In fact, The FCDA was in Cleveland during the All Star break hosting a 3-day industrial facilities protection seminar.

As reported in the *Plain Dealer*, representatives of more than 50 Cleveland area manufacturers were told, "The next war is expected to be one of great speed. There will be no time to rebuild or tool up.

If production stops, even for a short time, the war may be lost. If our target cities are struck with atomic weapons, the Department of Defense is planning to press into service all business organizations, or what is left of them, for the defense job."

The FCDA's most memorable contribution to the era, however, was the "Duck and Cover" drills for school children complete with a 9-minute video featuring Bert the Turtle, a cute amphibian who dives into his shell at the first sign of danger. The movie's message to children was anything but cute as the narrator described what to expect from a nuclear blast.

"There's a bright flash, brighter than the sun, brighter than anything you've ever seen. If you are not ready, do not know what to do, it can hurt you in different ways. It can knock you down hard or throw you against a tree or a wall. It is such a big explosion, it can smash in buildings and knock signboards over and break windows all over town. But if you duck and cover, like Bert, you'll be much safer. You know how bad sunburn can feel. The atomic bomb flash can burn you worse than a terrible sunburn, especially where you're not covered."

In 1954, the government was planning to install Nike missile sites in a number of American cities, including Cleveland. The purpose would be to shoot down Soviet bombers as a last-line-of-defense during an aerial attack. An FCDA poster at the time cited an Air Force claim that, "70 Out Of 100 Enemy Bombers Can Get Through," (how that figure was arrived at, or its accuracy, is not known.)

In the summer of 1954, Cleveland Mayor Anthony J. Celebrezze was actively arguing with the commander of the Army's 53rd Anti-aircraft Brigade over his choice of one of the seven Cleveland area locations for missile sites. The commander thought the city's beautiful Edgewater Park on Lake Erie, with a wooded bluff above and a beach below, would be a fine spot, a prospect that made the Italian-born Celebrezze's blood boil. In fact, he told the commander in July, "You might as well take my blood" as take the Edgewater location.

In the end, negotiation won out over confrontation and the nearly 50-acre missile site was installed at Lakefront Airport instead. A slender,

41-foot Nike missile in its launcher was in place by the summer of 1956, with more stored in underground magazines, and clearly visible from the city's Memorial Shoreway. Pointing toward the north, it was in position to shoot down Soviet bombers that in theory would be launched from Siberia and sweep over Canada and through the United States; Canadian fighter jets would be sent to intercept them. It was plausible that during the seventh inning stretch of a Cleveland Indian's game, Soviet bombers with a nuclear payload could come roaring in over Lake Erie. It was an age of fear.

Around 250 total Nike stations were constructed in the United States. The short-range capability of the original missile made it necessary that they be built in defensive rings around and very near population centers. New York City had 19 such sites. However by the late 1950s, the Soviets were placing emphasis on long-range missiles over bombers and by the mid-1960s, Nike bases were being phased out. Nike, the winged, Greek goddess of victory, is a word that now connotes something entirely more innocent in American culture.

On this All Star Tuesday, the *Atlanta Daily World*, an African-American newspaper, carried a baseball-related wire story from the ANP, the Associated Negro Press, a service that lasted from 1919-to-1964. The subhead, "Negro Baseball Dead in Chicago" summed up the story. Although the admission of black players to the major leagues 7 years earlier had been a significant step for both the players and the game, it was the worst thing that could have happened to Negro League baseball. Black fans now preferred major league teams, even if they had only one or two black players.

Writer Luix V. Overbea observed: "Sounding the death knell over Negro baseball here was the sad turnout for the July 4th doubleheader between the Indianapolis Clowns, best drawing card in Negro baseball, and the Kansas City Monarchs, NAL (Negro American League) champs (the game was played in Chicago's Comiskey Park). Both games were fast-moving and well-played, but only two or three thousand folks showed up. The weather was ideal, and on the North side, the Chicago Cubs were playing the St. Louis Cardinals, a team with a lone Negro pitcher. Thus there was no real competition. The fans just weren't interested. As I see it, fans here have become too White Sox conscious and want their baseball American league style. When the Sox are out of town, they go for the Brooklyn Dodgers and Jackie Robinson or the New York Giants and Willie Mays."

In West Virginia *The Charleston Daily Mail* gave an unusual appearance in that its nameplate, which almost always runs across the top of a newspaper's front page, ran about one-third of the way down. The upper space was given over to the All Star game, which was just in the third inning at press time. "2 Homers Give Stengel Stars Early Lead."

On an inside page, America's growing love affair with the automobile and the open road was evident in an ad for Hugh Stewart Motors, West Virginia's Largest Buick Dealer. Buick went with all V-8 engines in 1954 and the new Buick Special was "Honey on Wheels." The handsome, six-passenger sedan could be had for just $2,275.88, a bit smaller and less expensive than Buick's other models, and perfect for a young and growing family.

The Buick Special featured the carmaker's trademark, side portholes, a wide, toothy chrome grill that resembled a slightly turned down grin and General Motors' pointed, protruding twin front bumper mounts that became known as "Dagmars." The name derived from a busty TV and stage actress/comedienne of the day named Jenny Lewis who went by the single stage name of Dagmar. This Buick did not feature tailfins, however, as the 1950s "fin wars" between car manufacturers would not get underway in earnest for a couple of more years—a war "won" by Cadillac with the enormous and outrageous tailfins on its 1959 model.

The marriage of steel, chrome, and horsepower in 1950s automobiles meant that a collision could be a deadly one. Safety features such as seat belts were at least a decade from serious consideration—air bags hadn't been thought of—and dashboards then were made of metal and were unforgiving. Drum brakes provided inferior stopping power for these heavy cars compared to the disc brakes of today and America's increasingly crowded highways in 1954 remained overwhelmingly two-lane, providing little margin for error.

That concern for auto safety was reflected in the *Kingsport News* (Tennessee) where in the top corner of the front page was the statistic "Deathless Days," indicating the number of days since an automobile death in the city (1,020) and the county (22). It came with the reminder that, "Lives may be spared by a car kept repaired."

Located in the mountainous northeast corner of the state, Kingsport's elevation did not spare it from the heat wave as temperatures on Tuesday were supposed to touch 100 degrees. The hot news in town, however, was that a murder suspect had been picked up in nearby Virginia after killing a Kingston man while sticking up a local card game a couple of days earlier. It seems his victim was also his accomplice and one who had set the whole thing up. The suspect explained to police that the gun had gone off accidently as he became extremely nervous when the robbery got underway.

And in sports was a wire story recollection of a reporter named John Barrington who had grown up in rural Ohio—an Indians fan, had attended the 1935 All Star game in Cleveland as a youth, and now was there in the role of correspondent to cover the 1954 contest. "But this is a strictly personal footnote to All-Star history, a remembrance of what the All-Star game meant to one skinny, teen-aged, small-town kid … in this village, strung out along the two sides of the highway, you listened to the Indians games on the radio and read about them in the papers the noon bus dropped off in front of the general store."

"If you were a small boy, you could recite the Indians' batting averages by heart and you profoundly believed that some day you might be a big leaguer yourself. The really lucky ones were those who maybe once a year got to go the hundred miles or so to Cleveland and see a game. Before the (1935) All Star game, there was this one boy who didn't sleep for 2 weeks—or eat, either … he was too excited."

One thing haunted young Barrington in advance of the game, and that was forgetting or losing his ticket. So he put it in the overnight bag he would be taking and counted down the days. "Came the big day and the drive to Cleveland and time to unpack the bag. What bag? Father and son had assumed the other had put it in the car trunk." However, "stark tragedy" was avoided when Dad made a racing, 200- hundred-mile round trip back to town and rescued the ticket in time for the game.

As is Cleveland, a high profile death was on the minds of the good people of Chicago on this Tuesday: "Seek New Thorne Tests O.K." shouted the headline across the top of the *Chicago Daily Tribune*, as it was then known. The Thorne in question was department store heir Montgomery Ward Thorne, 20, who had died under mysterious circumstances 3 weeks earlier—a death that was national news as well.

"Monty," as he was called, had returned to Chicago after his freshman year of college at Fordham University in New York and gone not to his mother's luxury, 15-room apartment on East Lake Shore Drive but to a bohemian part of town where he rented a room. On June 19, he was found dead in bed, a total of nine needle marks in his arm, including four fresh ones, and evidence of heroin in the room. Had he lived to his 21st birthday in October, he would have shared in a $2.6 million dollar trust with his mother.

The matter became a staple of the front page when two Montgomery Ward Thorne wills surfaced—the original one that left all his money to his mother and a fresh one made nine days before his death that left much of it to his fiancée Maureen Ragen and her mother. Thorne had gone to his lawyer and made the change, telling him he didn't think he would live to collect his inheritance and to promise him a thorough investigation if he died young. He had told the Ragens he feared being poisoned by his mother's lawyer and that he believed she had already spent most of his inheritance.

Both Monty Thorne and Maureen Ragen had interesting lineages. Monty was the great-grandson of George R. Thorne who, with his brother-in-law, A. Montgomery Ward founded Montgomery Ward in 1872, a mail-order and later retail giant that at one time rivaled Sears in size and scope. Monty's father Gordon Thorne, grandson to George, was a three-times divorced playboy. He married a fourth time, a union that produced Monty, before dying at the age of 44, leaving an inheritance to his wife and son.

Maureen Ragen was the granddaughter of James Ragen, a Chicago Irish gang leader and street tough, who rose high in the-then shadowy world of racing news information. Before he found himself on the receiving end of a shotgun in 1946, he told authorities he feared that members of Al Capone's old syndicate were trying to muscle into his operation. He lingered in a hospital nearly 2 months after being shot, dying after apparently being given a secret injection of mercury.

Thorne's autopsy report concluded he had died from a mixture of morphine, barbiturates, and alcohol. However, the physician also added he "died by undue means. This definitely was not a natural death," which clearly implied the involvement of another and left more questions unanswered than answered. "Thorne Slain, Report Hints" read the headline atop the July 9, *Tribune*. A panel of four prominent pathologists subsequently reviewed the original autopsy report, which they found to be sketchy, and were requesting the body be exhumed for further testing.

The report of the four pathologists concluded that Thorne died not from an overdose but from pneumonia, a conclusion accepted by a coroner's jury at the end of the month. This did not end the controversy as the jury also recommended that the young man's unfortunate death continue to be investigated and the coroner's physician, who did the original autopsy, said he wouldn't sign the death certificate. "One group says he was a bad boy. Another group says he was a good boy. There has been nothing but confusion," he correctly observed.

Elsewhere in Chicago, the debut showing of an "Adults Only" Jane Russell film the previous weekend was causing headaches for the Cook County Sheriff Department. In drive-in theaters in rural parts of the county, hundreds of cars were being turned away by deputies and juvenile officers for containing occupants under the age of 21. The movie,

The French Line, which had been banned in the city of Chicago, was a bit of fluff plot-wise and designed primarily to show Ms. Russell, one of the most popular GI "pin-up girls" in World War II, in what was then considered to be a revealing, one-piece bathing suit that left film censors howling. The original script had called for a bikini—that would have been just too scandalous for its time. Ms. Russell recalled years later that she had tried on a bikini on the film set but that it had "horrified" the (presumably) all male film crew.

In sports, legendary *Tribune* Sports Editor Arch Ward was in Cleveland and had written a long column on the day's All Star game, a game born in his head 21 years earlier. In 1933, Chicago was looking for a sports component to go with its Century of Progress exposition, and it was Ward who came up with the idea of pulling in players from all over the country in mid-season for what was intended to be a one time "Dream Game." It was considered to be an impossible task by most, yet Ward, with the *Tribune* underwriting the costs, convinced baseball's management and team owners to go along. In that game, an aging Babe Ruth hit a two-run homer to carry the American League to victory before a packed stadium at Chicago's Comiskey Park and the contest has been an institution ever since. This would be Arch Ward's last All Star game, however, as he would die 3 days before the 1955 contest and be buried, fittingly, on the day of the game.

Seventh Inning

In the top of the seventh inning, Bob Porterfield still pitching, Alvin Dark fouled out to the catcher, Duke Snider lined a double to the left field corner for his third hit of the game, Stan Musial popped out to second base, and Ted Kluszewski grounded out to first. Score: American League 8, National League 7, in the middle of the seventh inning.

As fans stood for the seventh inning stretch, a tax-evasion trial was just underway less than a mile south of the stadium in the Federal Court building off Public Square involving a representative of Cleveland's immigrant tapestry, Shondor Birns. A baseball fan, Shondor, no doubt, would have rather been at the game, a hot dog in one hand and a beer in the other, perhaps. But he wasn't just any fan. He also carried the unofficial title—Cleveland's "Public Enemy No. 1."

Born Alexander Birnstein in 1905 in Austria-Hungary, Birns as it was later shortened, came to America as an infant, his parents stopping in New York briefly before coming to Cleveland. Times were hard and with the coming of Prohibition, Birns's mother took in a 10-gallon still to make whiskey for the local mob to help make ends meet. The still exploded and she was burned to death. Birns, after a stint in an orphanage, joined the Navy but was discharged for being underaged. He was now on his own, a young, but absolutely fearless, two-fisted tough, his given name Alexander having evolved into Shondor on the tongues of his immigrant, Italian and Jewish neighbors.

Birns was fascinated by the criminal life and on the streets of Cleveland, he received his education. Over the next 30 years he rose through the city's criminal ranks and murder, prostitution, numbers-running, protection, and bribery, to name some, would all appear on his resume. Although frequently arrested, nearly 100 times by one account, his witness and jury tampering skills kept him from serving much time.

Birns could be both utterly ruthless and absolutely charming; he craved respectability, and was on good terms with many on the police force and in the media. Leaving a Cleveland Indians game once, he flagged over two detectives assigned to follow him who then gave him a ride to his next destination—the detectives were later reprimanded. He also ran a couple of highly regarded restaurants over the years and he could count politicians and judges as customers. And many a newspaper reporter came away from a meeting with Birns with a free drink or two under his belt and good story to write. To many of Cleveland's working stiffs, he was larger than life—if not a hero.

On this day Birns, "a gambler with courtroom juries, according to the *Plain Dealer*, was in "the biggest gamble of his life." Well-prepared treasury agents were determined to nail him, some who had worked two years on the case, and who had a star witness. "Blonde Springs Trap for U.S. at Birns Trial," read a *Dealer* headline later in week. A former bookkeeper of Birns, whose good looks were as germane to the story as her testimony, testified she cooked the books she kept for him at one of his restaurants.

There would be no fixing this jury. He was convicted of three counts of income tax fraud and sentenced to 3 years, his longest sentence ever. While at county jail awaiting transfer to a federal prison, Birns occupied himself, "passing his time playing cards and listening to radio broadcasts of the ball games."

He was not out of prison long before going after a young numbers runner named Donald "The Kid" King who was rebelling against Birns' control of Cleveland's lucrative East Side numbers racket. When King's house was bombed in 1957, Birns was indicted for it, based on King's testimony, the latter surviving an assassination attempt before the trial began. The first jury hung but a scheduled second trial never took place as King feared for his life and decided not to cooperate.

In 1966, King was back in the news when he ran into a former employee of his who owed him money and, in a rage, literally stomped him to death in a Cleveland street. Fortune smiled on King, according to Cleveland lore, in the form of the well-greased palm of the judge assigned to the case and he served less than 4 years before going on to be better known as Don King, boxing promoter extraordinaire.

In 1968, Birns went back to federal prison for bribery and witness tampering, telling his young parole officer when he was released in 1971, "Kid, I don't break any provisions of parole. I'll tell you why. If I go back to jail, I'll die there." Birns became a somewhat mellowed, semiretired gangster in his golden years, playing handball and enjoying his daily routine visiting and holding court at several different bars and lounges.

On the evening of March 29, 1975, Holy Saturday, he visited one of those watering holes atop the west side of the Flats and shook hands and bought drinks for the house. After about an hour, he returned to his light blue, Lincoln Continental Mark IV, his last act in this world. The earth shuddered, flames shot into the night sky and thunder roared through the Cuyahoga Valley as one of the most powerful car bombs Cleveland police ever investigated blew the car, and Shondor Birns, to pieces. The blast was so great that some of the debris landed on St. Malachi Catholic Church about 1,000 feet away where more than 100 waited for evening Mass.

Cleveland police spent much of the night gathering his remains and the next day, people in their Easter clothes picked through what was left of the rubble for souvenirs. No one was ever arrested or charged for the murder and an editorial in *The Cleveland Press* concluded, "The cold truth about Shondor is that the world is better off without a man who brought tragedy to so many others." That day in March became known as, "The day they blew Shondor away."

In New Orleans, heat and humidity were hardly news, but the torrid pennant race between the New Orleans Pelicans and the Atlanta

Crackers of the Southern Association was. "Those rampaging Pelicans swept a doubleheader from the (Birmingham) Barons with the greatest of ease Monday …" reported *The Times-Picayune*. They were also happy there that popular ex-Pelican Frank Thomas, of the Pittsburgh Pirates, had been selected as an All Star game reserve. Thomas let out a yell in the Pirates locker room when notified of his selection and said, "I was going as a spectator on my own. Now I'll go and take my wife along. It's the greatest thing that ever happened to me."

The race between the Pelicans and Crackers in 1954 would go to the wire, Atlanta edging New Orleans by two games. The Crackers then went on to beat the Houston Buffaloes in the Dixie Series, a postseason title series between the Southern Association and the Texas League that began in 1920. But change loomed on the horizon for minor league baseball. The Dixie Series would be played for the last time in 1958, the Pelicans would turn off the locker room lights for the final time after the 1960 season, and the Southern Association (SA) would be no more after 1961.

The death of the SA meant the beginning of the end for one of the more quaint minor league ball ballparks ever, Sulphur Dell, home to the Nashville Vols. Baseball was first played at the lowland spot by Union soldiers during the Civil War, and a stadium was built in 1885. Sportswriter Grantland Rice, then in Nashville, christened it Sulphur Dell in 1908 because of the sulphur spring that bubbled nearby. Squeezed into a tight, city block, only 26 feet separated third base and the grandstand.

The infield was below street level and in the outfield, an embankment rose sharply to meet the fence in the very short right field area. There atop the slope, or shelf as it was called, the outfielder stood more than 22 feet above the level of home plate if he was back by the fence, which hitters could reach with ease. Many right fielders positioned themselves partway down the bank and were characterized by one sportswriter as mountain goats. And more than a few slipped and tumbled down it when chasing a ball. Sulphur Dell fell to the wrecking ball in 1969 and its outfield summit was leveled. The site is now a parking lot for nearby Tennessee State Capitol buildings.

The plunge in Southern Association attendance, from a high of 2.2 million in 1947 to under 800,000 in 1960, largely reflected the minor league baseball experience in the 1950s. The primary culprit was television, which not only brought major league baseball into living rooms but offered a variety of other entertainment choices as well—alternatives to heading for the town ball ballpark.

An official with the AA Eastern League was in Cleveland for the All Star game, explaining to reporters the carnival-like promotions he was forced to engage in to get people out to ball games: "The other night in Elmira I even shot a man out of a coffin at second base." In the modern-day minor league baseball landscape, promotions are as much a part of the game as balls and strikes.

Coming into the game for the American League in the bottom of the seventh inning was Chicago White Sox second baseman Nellie Fox. A Christmas Day baby born in 1927, Fox broke in with the Philadelphia Athletics in 1947 and was traded to Chicago after the 1949 season—and there his career blossomed. For the next 13 years, teaming first with shortstop and fellow All Star Chico Carrasquel, then his even more talented replacement and eventual Hall of Fame selectee, Luis Aparicio, Fox was half one of the slickest, surest, double-play combinations in major league history.

A diminutive man with little power, Fox could not hope for the majestic home run, but led the league in singles 7 years straight. Not a glamorous statistic, but it's usually a single that starts a rally or keeps one going. He would have his best year in 1959, winning the American League Most Valuable Player Award in leading the White Sox to their first pennant in 40 years. He played until 1965 then coached for some years after that. In 1975, he died of cancer at the too young age of 47; Fox always had a wad of chewing tobacco in his mouth.

He did not live long enough to see his own selection to the Hall of Fame or the statue of him with arm outstretched forever, making the quick flip to Aparicio, also in bronze, on the Champions Plaza in the stadium where the White Sox now play. Here in the baseball field of the mind, Aparicio takes the flip from Fox at the second base bag, snatches the ball from his glove, leaps high above the spikes and dust of the runner sliding in and fires a perfect strike to first base to complete a classic 4–6–3 double play, baseball ballet, before the two trot together off a mist-shrouded field.

Remaining in the game to pitch for the National League in the bottom of the seventh inning was Marv Grissom who would have an easy time of it. Nellie Fox led off and did something he did very little of in his career, which was strike out; teammate Chico Carrasquel grounded out to shortstop, and Ted Williams struck out for the second straight time, perhaps cursing one of the deities in a most sacrilegious manner—something he did almost as well as hitting as he walked back to the dugout. Score: American League 8, National League 7, at the end of seven innings.

In the Big Sky country of Montana, *The Billings Gazette* told of an area ranch hand who laid 12 hours in the broiling sun with two broken legs before being found. The horse fell on the hand's leg, breaking it, and when he tried to remount, it kicked him, breaking the other before running off. In other matters local, thieves broke down a Billings tavern door and then used it to carry off about two dozen cases of beer. The bar owner estimated the brew's value at $90.

In issues more far-ranging, page one featured of a photo of Rep. Walter Judd of Minnesota, a staunch anticommunist, who warned that the United States must form a NATO-type alliance with Asian countries or "go down like a house of cards." Years later after he was out of office, Judd would telephone the White House to urge then President Reagan not to meet with Communist Party General Secretary Mikhail Gorbachev of the Soviet Union as tensions were easing between the two powers. The president reportedly refused to take his call.

Earlier in the year, Judd had been a hero when Puerto Rican nationalists opened fire in the House of Representatives on March 1. Five congressmen were wounded including Alvin M. Bentley of Michigan who took a bullet near his heart. Despite the situation still being

newsman Mike Wallace and his actress wife, Buff Cobb. Radio shows hosted by married couples were popular in the day and focused more on chit chat and sponsor product promotion than on substance. Wallace would go on to tackle substantive issues for decades on the CBS Television show *60 Minutes,* which began in 1968.

On a sadder note, a coroner's jury sat the previous day to begin the process of declaring legally dead a Sitka boy who had disappeared the previous summer from a small boat up the coast at Pelican, but whose body had never been found.

In Milwaukee, professional baseball was in its second season after the Braves had moved there from Boston in 1953. The Milwaukee Brewers were the Braves top minor league team at the time and the organization moved the team to Toledo, which had recently lost its minor league franchise to Charleston, West Virginia.

The team was renamed the Glass Sox, after the city's glass industry, and played its games in Swayne Field, an aging but intimate double-deck stadium located in a neighborhood near downtown. Casey Stengel cut his managerial teeth for 6 years there, his first skipper job after leaving the majors. He led the 1927 Toledo Mud Hens to the Junior World Series title, pinch hitting and playing the outfield on occasion.

The Braves took advantage of the All Star break to travel to Toledo for its annual exhibition game against its top farm team. The Braves won the Monday evening contest 6–1 but the big story, in the sports pages of the *Milwaukee Journal,* was the player whose 1951 "shot heard 'round the world" home run broke Brooklyn's heart, Bobby Thomson. He had been acquired by the Braves in a major, off-season trade, but broke his ankle during the first spring training game and had yet to see action.

Thomson came to the plate in the exhibition game as a pinch-hitter and slammed the first pitch he saw high over Swayne Field's 400-foot, left-center field wall.

Thomson was all smiles as he ran around the bases, still limping a bit. And even though it was only an exhibition game, he was mobbed by his teammates when he reached the dugout.

Also with the Braves in Toledo was one of the great third base-men to play the game, Eddie Mathews, pictured in the *Toledo Blade* surrounded by kids and signing autographs. After leading the National League in home runs with 47 the previous year and being hailed as the next Babe Ruth, he was left off this year's All Star team after a slow start. Mathews would not miss another All Star game in his Hall of Fame career until 1964. He would be the only Brave to play in all three cities the franchise was located; Boston, Milwaukee and Atlanta.

The Braves, Glass Sox, and Swayne Field would not last. The Glass Sox left for Wichita, Kansas in 1956, after which the stadium was razed and replaced by a shopping center of the same name; the Braves left for Atlanta in 1965. Baseball would before long return permanently to Milwaukee in the form of the major league Brewers and to Toledo which got back its Mud Hens—both teams now settled in fine, new downtown stadiums. In Toledo, the purists know that behind the now time-worn shopping center, a crumbling concrete wall remains from the original ball park where Casey Stengel once roamed.

About a hundred miles to the east, former Indians owner Bill Veeck was in Cleveland for the game: "Magnetic Bill Veeck Tells Host of Friends Los Angeles is Next," read the *Milwaukee Journal* headline. A raconteur if the game of baseball ever saw one, Veeck was holding court for a stream of visitors, particularly members of the media who knew a quote machine when they heard one. He was now in the employ of the Chicago Cubs and thinking about his next team, his eye on the lucrative, and as yet untapped, market of Los Angeles.

Veeck had a reputation as a maverick and a promoter extraordi-naire. When he owned the minor league Milwaukee Brewers in the 1940s, his fan giveaways included orchids, birds, a 200-pound block of ice, and a horse. He even tried morning games for workers coming off third shift. In Cleveland, when his Indians were eliminated from the 1949 race, he arranged a mock funeral before a night game to bury their 1948 World Series flag behind the centerfield fence, complete with hearse, pallbearers, and flowers. He played it to the hilt, stand-ing with a top hat and daubing away at imaginary tears during the "service."

Although it had been only 7 years and a week since Veeck signed Larry Doby as the first black player in the American League, he had already owned, and sold two teams—the Indians in 1949 after an expensive divorce, and the St. Louis Browns to a group in Baltimore where they became the Orioles at the end of the 1953 season. If the 1947 signing of Doby could be said to be an act of the sublime, then the ridiculous came with the Browns in 1951.

The Browns were a sad sack team, playing in front of empty seats and in the long shadow of the Cardinals. To bring in folks for a Sunday doubleheader against Detroit, Veeck promised entertainment galore to honor both the American League, which was celebrating its 50th anniversary, and Falstaff Brewing, which was also having a birthday. As the largest crowd in 4 years entered the turnstiles, they were given a slice of birthday cake, a box of ice cream, and a can of Falstaff Beer.

Veeck had gotten Falstaff on board as a sponsor of the day promising the company national publicity when it was all over. After the first game there were jugglers, clowns, a band, and an antique car parade and, to top it off, a giant birthday cake was wheeled out on the field and out popped a dwarf named Eddie Gaedel, complete with elf slippers and a uniform with the number 1/8 on his back. The Falstaff executives groaned, feeling they had been conned—national publicity from such a trite stunt indeed. Veeck expressed a feigned regret, but he was far from finished.

The second game got underway and the Browns manager sent a pinch hitter to the plate in the first inning to hit for the leadoff batter, highly unusual by itself, but even more so because it was Gaedel, all 3 feet, 7 inches and 65 pounds of him, swinging a toy bat. The home plate umpire stopped the game and demanded to see the contract of the diminutive slugger, but Veeck had his bases covered. He had signed Eddie and mailed the paperwork the previous day, knowing it wouldn't reach league offices in time. After a delay and with the crowd absolutely howling, the umpire motioned the vertically challenged pinch hitter to the plate. Veeck's plan was in place and his only fear was that Gaedel, who was a bit of a ham, would actually swing at the ball against his strictest orders.

Detroit's catcher gave it his best shot, getting on his knees to try to give his pitcher a target but it was no use. The hurler was almost in hysterics as balls three and four sailed well over Eddie's head; he had resisted the urge to swing, and he trotted to first base, stopping twice to bow deeply along the way. Replaced by a pinch runner, he left the field to a standing ovation while the Falstaff people pounded Veeck on the back.

In no mood to cheer was American League President Will Harridge who was furious and who voided the contract the next day, accusing Veeck of making a mockery of the game. Newspapers around the country ripped him as well but he didn't care. He had promised something out of the ordinary and he had delivered. He had hoped the walk to Eddie would have turned out to be the winning run but the Browns lost the game, one of 102 that year.

Gaedel, a baseball fan, had a blast, telling reporters after the game, "For a minute I felt like Babe Ruth" while standing at the plate. Baseball was eventually forgiving of the whole thing and his number 1/8 uniform has been displayed in the Hall of Fame. And he remains the only dwarf to have ever batted in a major league baseball game, a distinction it's very unlikely he'll ever share.

Veeck eventually got back in the ownership game, heading a group that bought a controlling interest in the Chicago White Sox in 1959 and, using his promotional acumen, the team set attendance records for the next 2 years. Poor health forced him back out of the game in 1961. He was rebuffed in his attempts to get an American League franchise in the Los Angeles area, and it appeared his baseball days were over. But he had one more baseball run left in him, coming back as White Sox owner in 1975. He also had one more legendary promotion left in him, Disco Demolition Night in 1979.

Playing on the resentment that rock and roll fans then had toward disco music, Veeck's son Mike teamed with a local, antidisco rock radio station and offered admission to a July evening doubleheader for 98 cents—the station's call numbers were 97.9—in exchange for a disco record album, all of which would be placed in a large crate and blown up in center field by a station deejay between games. Expecting a crowd of about 12,000, White Sox officials were unprepared for the huge and heartily partying throng, records, and antidisco banners in hand, that packed Comiskey Park to the rafters while thousands more milled outside.

The crate filled up quickly and many in the stands, still with record albums in hand, realized they also made for fine Frisbees—soon vinyl discs sailed about the stadium. When the central event occurred after the first game and explosives sent records flying into the air, thousands poured out of the stands, running about the field while the stadium lights beamed through a layer of smoke that lingered overhead in as bizarre a scene that ever occurred in baseball.

Some fed a fire where the explosion had taken place, others took the bases and chunks of the field as souvenirs, while still others climbed the foul poles. Police in riot gear eventually restored order. There were a handful of minor injuries. A smoldering hole in the centerfield grass left the field unplayable and the second game was forfeited. If the Eddie Gaedel promotion had gone exactly as planned, this one had blown up in every sense of the word.

Veeck sold the White sox in 1981 and retired to the role of the fan, spending many a summer day in the bleachers at Wrigley Field watching the Cubs. His father had been president of the team from 1919-to-1933 and as a youngster, Bill had worked as a ticket seller, vendor, and junior groundskeeper. As a young adult he worked as club treasurer and in 1937 planted the legendary ivy that now covers Wrigley's outfield walls. He had one day hoped to own the Cubs but that never happened.

Crazy promotions aside, he left a larger mark on the game. Out of his creative mind came such baseball standards as exploding scoreboards, Bat Day, names on the backs of uniforms and fan giveaways of all kinds. And in retrospect, his burial of the Indians 1948 World Series flag was visionary; Cleveland hasn't won a World Series since.

Eighth Inning

Coming into the game in the top of the eighth inning to pitch for the American League was Bob Keegan of the Chicago White Sox, making his only All Star game appearance. He played collegiately for the Bucknell University Bison and served in World War II afterward. He signed with the Yankees organization in 1946 and bounced around, finally making it the major leagues in 1953 with Chicago at the advanced age, for baseball, of 32. This All Star appearance was a highlight of his professional career, the other being a no-hitter he twirled in 1957 before retiring the following year. He is enshrined in the Bucknell Hall of Fame along with fellow Bison, and one of baseball's greatest pitchers ever, Christy Mathewson.

Also coming into the game for American League in this frame was Washington Senators pitcher Dean Stone, the onetime pride of the Erie, Pennsylvania, Sailors of the Middle Atlantic League (MAL). Dozens of minor leagues and their teams with colorful nicknames once dotted the American landscape and the MAL was no exception.

Also in Pennsylvania at one time or another were the Beaver Falls Beavers, the Altoona Engineers, the Uniontown Coal Barons, the Johnstown Johnnies, the Scottdale Scotties, and the Charleroi Babes. Has any other professional sports team composed of men gone by that moniker? In Ohio, there were the Springfield Chicks, the Dayton Ducks, the Youngstown Tubers, and the Youngstown Gremlins.

West Virginia featured the Wheeling Stogies, the Parkersburg Parkers, and the Beckley Black Knights while New York had the Niagara Falls Frontiers and the Lockport Locks.

Although he led the league in walks, Stone also helped lead the Erie team to the Middle Atlantic League pennant in 1951. After that year, both the league, and the Sailors, sailed into baseball history. Stone reached the major leagues late in the 1953 season with Washington and 1954 found him playing, as a rookie, in what would be his only All Star game as substitute for the injured Ferris Fain of Chicago. He would play for a total of six major league teams before finishing up in Japan in 1964.

Coming into the game for the National League in the top of eighth was one of a number of sluggers who played for the Cincinnati Reds in the 1950s, outfielder Gus Bell, playing in his second of four All Star games. Like Ray Boone who was also playing this day, Bell would also be part of a three-generation baseball family although he couldn't have known it at the time. His son Buddy Bell would play in the same stadium as a popular third baseman for the Indians and appear in five All Star games with Cleveland and with Texas while Buddy's sons, Mike and David Bell, would also reach the major leagues.

In the top of the eighth inning with Bob Keegan pitching for the American League, Randy Jackson grounded out to short and Willie Mays singled to centerfield. Roy Campanella struck out and Gus Bell came to the plate to hit for the pitcher, Marv Grissom, and slammed a shot over the right centerfield fence for a two-run homer. Red Schoendienst lifted a fly ball to right that Minnie Minoso dropped after a long run for a two-base error and Alvin Dark grounded an infield single to third base, Schoendienst moving to third and sliding under the tag of Ray Boone. That was all for Bob Keegan; Dean Stone came in to pitch.

Up came the dangerous Duke Snider but Schoendienst was hardly a spectator at third. On a one and one count, Red broke for home going for one of the rarest, and boldest, plays in baseball: the steal of home plate. Perhaps he thought the rookie Stone would be nervous and distracted but instead he fired a strike to catcher Yogi Berra who tagged him out. But the National League players and coaches thought Stone had balked and what followed was a good old-fashioned rhubarb—baseball vernacular for argument.

Leading the way was New York Giants Manager Leo Durocher who was coaching at third base for the National League and who absolutely exploded. Durocher's nickname was "The Lip" and he lived up to it as he charged home plate and put on a foot-stomping, dirt-kicking, arm-waving, profanity-laced beauty of a baseball tirade while the fans in the stands in Cleveland howled and hooted. However in what was, according to the *Plain Dealer,* "his most violent field demonstration in a long while," was also to no avail; the call stood and the inning came to a wild end. Score: National League 9, American League 8 in the middle of the eighth inning.

If it was hot in Cleveland, then it was scorching in St. Louis, a city southern in locale by comparison. "No Relief in Sight Following Second Hottest Day in History of St. Louis" read the headline on page one of the *St. Louis Post Dispatch.* The temperature had shot up to 109.3 degrees the previous day and stayed above 100 until 9 P.M. and above 90 until 2 A.M. This sent many families fleeing out of doors to sleep. One couple and their two young daughters, pictured on the grounds of the city's Forest Park, were stretched out in the dark on blankets.

On an inside page were a couple of syndicated columns by Roscoe Drummond of the *New York Herald Tribune,* who covered politics in the United States for 50 years, and by Doris Fleeson of *The New York Daily News,* who was the country's first female syndicated columnist. Fleeson was covering the Governors' Conference in New York, which she referred to as a "seed bed" for possible future presidential candidates. She lamented the generally dullish group gathered there, wishing there was "an amusing demagogue" to write about.

Drummond was responding to recent calls by some politicians for less television coverage of themselves and of the political process. After the recently concluded and televised Army-McCarthy hearings, Vice-President Richard Nixon had written in *The Federal Bar Journal* of the "circus atmosphere" created by television. Wrote Drummond, "Television doesn't create a 'circus atmosphere'—it only records a circus atmosphere when it has been created by others."

Wishing for less future television coverage of politics was futile. Perhaps the Vice-President knew early on that the probing lens of the television camera and the heat of the lights were never going to be his friend. Over the next 20 years in his television appearances in roles as a candidate then eventually as president, Nixon often appeared ill at ease.

In sports, "Nationals 9, Americans 8, After 7 1/2 Innings" ran the headline across the top of the page. The game in Cleveland ran past the deadline of the afternoon *Post-Dispatch* so they went with what they had. This included a game story by one of their sportswriters and a United Press Telephoto of Al Rosen being greeted at home plate by Bobby Avila and Yogi Berra after hitting his first home run.

There's no good way to die, but passing away suddenly when doing something you love is probably as good a deal as one can get. Elmer (Si) Stilwell was a wiry man with a crinkle-eyed smile who was delivering the play-by-play of the game not with his voice but with the touch of his talented finger. Si was one of a dwindling number of morse code operators left in the country and was sending the game in morse for United Press back to their New York office. Stilwell, according to *The Cleveland Press*, "first heard the click-click of a telegrapher's key in 1914 and it was like enchanting music to him." He had worked the Western Union wire at ball games for nearly 20 years and the stadium press box in Cleveland was like a second home to him. He always got a kick out of the fact he could watch a ball game while working at the same time. This All Star game was his last assignment; during the game he collapsed and died on the press box floor of an apparent heart attack. He was 63.

In Abilene, Texas, this All Star Tuesday it was, what else—hot—according to the evening edition of *The Abilene Reporter-News*. The temperature had passed the 100 degree mark before noon on its way to a predicted record high of 105, although not quite the 110 in Dallas County to the east the previous day that had a local cowman claiming he could "smell the grass burning in the pastures."

A matter much more serious was at hand in Abilene's 104th District Court where a motion for change of venue was being heard. Ex-convict Bill Gaither had been charged with murder with malice for killing 27-year-old Abilene Officer Jimmy Spann, a married father of two young children, in a wild gun battle about a month earlier. Gaither himself had been shot and seriously wounded in the incident. His lawyer was requesting transfer of the case to another county given the amount degree of prejudice toward his client that existed locally. Gaither was eventually convicted and received a 99-year sentence.

In sports, "Stengel Confident of All Star Win" read one headline while in more mundane baseball matters The Abilene Blue Sox had been clobbered by the Albuquerque Dukes 13–4 the day before in West Texas–New Mexico League action. The Blue Sox were without the services of their young shortstop, Ray Ellison, who had been hit in the head by a pitch the previous Sunday in Pampa where he was, "resting comfortably but still woozy" in a local hospital—this in the days before players wore batting helmets.

The West Texas–New Mexico was a Class C League that consisted mostly of independent, non-major league affiliated teams designed to entertain rather than groom talent. High scoring games were the rule as teams played in higher altitude towns where hot winds swept through bandbox ballparks and the players traveled dusty roads in old busses and station wagons, playing for a few bucks and the love of the game. That dust settled for good after the 1955 season when the league went out of business.

In other sports news, the Texas State Negro Golf Association had opened play in its annual tournament on the municipal course in Abilene that morning. Local organizers were disappointed over the turnout of only 40 golfers compared to 200 the year before in San Antonio, blaming the greater driving distance to Abilene and the baking West Texas heat for the decline.

On this sweltering All Star Tuesday, the local grocery store chain of Pick -N- Pay Supermarkets was having a "Snowballs in July" promotion.

The store had gathered, and frozen, thousands of them from a storm that had buried the Cleveland area the previous March and anyone in a store checkout line when a special bell rang received a prize and a snowball, in a plastic bag. The store had also sent boxes of these snowballs as gifts to both President Dwight D. Eisenhower in Washington and former President Harry S. Truman in Missouri who was recovering from surgery. What the present and former leaders of the free world did with them, or why they would have wanted them in the first place, is unknown.

Coming into the game for the National League in the bottom of the eighth was Philadelphia Phillies catcher Smoky Burgess replacing Roy Campanella who was richly entitled to a rest; after all, it had been years since he'd had a break. He had crouched behind the plate for the National League every single All Star inning since the seventh inning of the 1948 game, 55 consecutively in all.

Forrest Harrill Burgess, who somewhere along the way acquired the classic baseball nickname of Smoky, was playing in his first of what would be six All Star games. A solid catcher, he became known for his ability to pinch-hit, a manager's dream, his 145 hits in the pinch standing as a major league record for a time until subsequently passed by three others. He played for five teams in an 18-year career, picking up a World Series ring when he was with the Pittsburgh Pirates in 1960.

Also coming into the game for the National League in the bottom of the eighth inning was Milwaukee Brave pitcher Gene Conley, playing in his first of what would be three All Star games. During baseball's off season, players occupy themselves in a variety of ways but Conley's was unique. A 6-foot, 8-inch reserve forward/center, he spent his winters playing professionally in the National Basketball Association.

He could count as teammates baseball stars like Hank Aaron in Milwaukee and basketball stars like Bill Russell of the Boston Celtics, one of two NBA teams Conley played for. As part of the World Series title Braves in 1957 and the NBA champion Celtic teams of 1959-to-1961, he is the only athlete to win championships in two major American sports. Two weeks after the Celtics title in 1961, he pitched the Boston Red Sox, the last of four teams he played for, to a victory over the Washington Senators and drove in a run; sitting in the stands in Fenway Park were Celtic teammates Russell and K. C. Jones.

Also coming into the game for the National League in the bottom of the eighth inning was Brooklyn Dodgers first baseman Gil Hodges, playing in his sixth consecutive of what would be a total of eight All Star games. One of the anchors of the good Dodgers teams of the 1950s, he was also extremely popular and it is said that he was the only Dodgers player the Ebbetts Field fans would not boo. He finished the 1952 season in a brutal batting slump going 0 for 34, 21 of those hitless at bats coming in the World Series against the Yankees. When the slump carried over into the following season, fans responded by sending letters of encouragement and gifts and tokens for good luck. One fan, Father Herbert Redmond of Brooklyn's St. Francis Catholic Church, took it to a higher level when he told his congregation, "It's far too hot for a homily. Keep the Commandments and say a prayer for Gil Hodges."

Also coming into the game for the National League in the bottom of the eighth inning was another Dodger, pitcher Carl Erskine making his only All Star game appearance. Erskine didn't just play in Brooklyn, he was one of the Dodger players who lived there too. An actual part of the community who would work with youngsters at the local ball diamonds, he was affectionately known as "Ersk" which often came out as "Oisk" in the local lingo known as Brooklynese.

Erskine broke in with the Dodgers in 1948 and played his entire 12-year career for them, the last two in Los Angeles. In retirement he returned to his native Indiana and eventually became president of a bank. He later wrote two books regarding his Dodgers days; *Tales From the Dodgers Dugout* and *What I learned From Jackie Robinson*. He and Robinson were good friends.

Coming into the game for the American League in the bottom of the eighth inning was Washington Senators first baseman Mickey Vernon playing in his fourth of seven All Star games, albeit this one as a substitute for injured White Sox third baseman George Kell. It was Vernon's .337 batting average the previous year that nosed out the Indian's Al Rosen's .336, thus preventing Rosen from winning the Triple Crown.

On Opening Day in Washington earlier in the year, Vernon was presented with a silver bat for his batting title by President Eisenhower who then stayed and watched the game. In the bottom of the tenth inning, Vernon belted a game-winning home run and when he rounded third, was surprised to see a man in a suit standing among the players waiting to greet him at home plate. It was a Secret Service agent who took him over to the presidential box where a grinning president stuck out his hand and said, "Nice going."

Vernon was a fine first baseman and, both quiet and charismatic, one of the more well-liked players in the game. But he had the misfortune of spending 13 years of his 20-year career with the Washington Senators, a team that typically hovered near the bottom of the American League standings." His fortune came as a coach with the 1960 Pittsburgh Pirates who won the World Series over the Yankees giving him a World Series ring. He then managed the expansion Senators in 1961 and 1962, 100-loss seasons each, before moving on part of the way into the 1963 campaign. Although not in the Hall of Fame, many of the players of his era think he ought to be.

Also coming into the game for the American League was Cleveland Indians outfielder Larry Doby playing in his sixth straight of what would be seven All Star games. At the end of September, 1946, Lawrence Eugene Doby trotted off Ruppert Field in Newark, New Jersey, a champion as the Newark Eagles of the Negro American League had defeated the Kansas City Monarchs to win the Colored World Series. At about the same time around 400 miles to the north, Jackie Robinson was trotting off the field in Delormier Stadium in Montreal, a champion having led the Montreal Royals of the International League to the Little Word Series title. Both players were clearly of major league caliber but blocked by social forces they could not control, were forced to play for minor titles.

All that changed the following season when Jackie Robinson stepped on the field on Opening Day for the Brooklyn Dodgers. The National League was finally integrated and it was time for the American League to step up. On July 4, 1947, Doby walked off Ruppert Field for the last time and took a long train ride that took him from an old world to a new one. He had been acquired by the Indians and was to meet the team in Chicago in time for their game there the next day.

Jackie Robinson played a year in Brooklyn's farm system and had long, preparatory conversations with team owner Branch Rickey before joining the majors. Larry Doby's introduction was a bit different. He arrived at Comiskey Park, met Cleveland owner Bill Veeck for the first time in a White Sox office, signed a contract, then was sent to the locker room to meet his new teammates, with Veeck's admonition that, "a baseball player is judged on one basis only, what he does with his bat and his glove." If only it were that easy.

In the Cleveland locker room, manager Lou Boudreau had lined up the players in front of their lockers to meet their new teammate. Larry stopped at each locker and extended his hand. A few extended theirs in return; many didn't. Then it was to the dugout to sit with two plainclothes policemen Veeck had hired, just in case. This was Larry Doby's abrupt, and chilly, welcome to the major leagues.

Fifty years later when Jackie Robinson was posthumously, and justly, honored for breaking baseball's color barrier, the still-living Doby was virtually ignored by the media. Yet as the first black player to step on the field in a number of American League stadiums he, like Jackie, had to endure verbal abuse from fans, players, coaches and managers with the death threats both had received weighing on their minds.

Virtually all the threats of death or violence made toward Robinson and Doby at the time were the empty words of cowardly minds. However they both had to carry the fear that the person walking a little too quickly toward them in the stadium parking lot or following a little too closely in a car on the way home from a game, could be the one exception.

Doby didn't play that much the rest of 1947, appearing mostly as a pinch hitter and defensive replacement. He was an infielder and Cleveland's infield was already set. However his Hall of Fame career took off in 1948 when he moved to center field and batted .301 and helped drive the Indians to the pennant and World Series. In game four of the Series, Doby slammed a home run, the first ever World Series roundtripper by a black player, and one that proved to be the margin of victory in a 2–1 Cleveland win, Tribe pitcher Steve Gromek going all the way.

After the game Gromek, a Polish boy from Hamtramck, Michigan, whose ancestors had come to America as immigrants and Doby, an urban lad from Paterson, New Jersey, whose ancestors had come over as slaves, were photographed in the locker room grinning ear-to-ear and hugging cheek-to-cheek, faces pressed together in a moment of pure jubilation. For all the people of good faith and good heart at the time who knew that integrating baseball was the right thing to do, this picture spoke a thousand words, if not 10 times that.

Doby became the premier centerfielder in the American League in the late 1940s and the early 1950s, until a kid named Mickey Mantle came along, leading the American League in home runs in 1952 and again in 1954. Doby's quiet, workman-like approach to the game made him popular with Cleveland fans.

Fifty years and almost to the day of his breaking the color barrier in the American league, Doby again stood on a baseball field in Cleveland, this time on the pitchers mound in Jacobs Field to throw out the ceremonial first pitch in the 1997 All Star game. He acknowledged before he died that he didn't get anywhere near the attention that Jackie Robinson did, despite going through the same things, but said that he had no regrets or hard feelings; the only thing he really cared about was playing baseball at the major league level and that was what he got to do.

The relationship between Larry Doby and Bill Veeck transcended that of owner/player and the two became good friends. Doby once said that he hoped that his father, who had died when he was eight, would have been like Bill Veeck had he lived. Veeck's signing of Larry Doby was not just out of a need for a centerfielder; he truly saw the injustice of discrimination and was involved in Civil Rights causes in later years. In 1978 Veeck, then owner of the Chicago White Sox, hired Doby to manage the team, making him baseball's second black manager.

In the bottom of the eighth inning with the lanky Gene Conley pitching for the National League, Minnie Minoso grounded out to shortstop and Larry Doby came to the plate to pinch hit for the pitcher Dean Stone. A murmur echoed through the crowd that quickly rose into a low roar as hometown favorite Doby, who would go on to win the American League home run title, stepped into the batter's box. Seventeen runs had been scored in the game to this point and there was no reason for the fans to think the scoring was over. Doby took a vicious cut at a Conley fastball and laced a line drive to left-center field. Willie Mays raced back but ran out of room as the ball sailed far over the fence. The Municipal Stadium crowd exploded as Doby circled the bases and was greeted at home plate by Mickey Mantle and Yogi Berra who were waiting to bat. The game was now tied.

Gene Conley, playing in his first All Star game and with the crowd still roaring, perhaps became rattled as Mickey Mantle lined a single to center and Yogi Berra dropped a single into short left field. Hitting hero of the day Al Rosen, who already had two homers on the day, drew a walk and the bases were loaded. National League Manager Walter Alston had seen enough and brought in Carl Erskine to pitch. Mickey Vernon came to the plate and took a called third strike, and it looked like Erskine might get out of the inning.

Baseball, perhaps more than the other major league sports, can at times reward failure and punish success. A pitcher can make a great pitch, the batter can take a lousy swing, but if it's a "seeing eye" ground ball that dribbles between two infielders, or a weak pop up that drops between the infielder charging out and the outfielder charging in, it's a hit. Statistically, the pitcher failed.

On the other hand, the pitcher can make a lousy pitch and the batter can hit a line drive as hard as one can be humanly hit, but if it's right at a fielder who makes the catch, it's a routine out. Statistically, the batter failed. Few balls in World Series history have been hit as hard as the one Cleveland's Vic Wertz hit in game one in 1954 that Willie Mays, using both his excellent speed and the unusual dimensions of the Polo Grounds, turned into an out. That ball would have been an easy home run in most of the other stadiums of the day and any built since 1960. However the statistical record will always show that Vic Wertz came to the plate and failed.

So it was in the bottom of the eighth inning in Cleveland on July 13, 1954, in the sometimes arbitrary game of baseball and in the 21st All

Star game ever played that Chicago's Nellie Fox came to the plate with the bases loaded and two out. Fox had struck out his previous at bat, a rarity for him, and was determined to get his bat on the ball.

In this game dominated by home runs and long, extra base hits, Fox swung and fought off an Erskine fastball and lofted the kind of ball toward the shortstop Alvin Dark that has been variously been called over the years a bleeder, a blooper, a looper, a flare, a dying quail, and a Texas Leaguer; in other words, a weakly struck ball that, in a fair world, would not be a hit. Dark raced back as fast as he could but the ball bounced softly in the outfield grass just beyond his reach. Mickey Mantle and Yogi Berra, who with two out were off with the crack of the bat, came charging home to score to give the American League an 11–9 lead and the stadium shook. Carl Erskine had made a good pitch but the statistical record will always show that he failed. Chico Carrasquel came to the plate and popped out to the shortstop to finish off the inning but the damage had been done. Score: American League 11, National League 9, after eight innings.

On this All Star Tuesday the number one hit single on the music charts in the country was "Little Things Mean a Lot" by Kitty Kallen. She was a big band singer in the 1940s who made a comeback with a brief solo career in the 1950s. The song, which stayed at number one for 10 weeks, was standard for its day, a sweet and sentimental love lyric recorded with orchestral accompaniment.

But a music revolution was underway, although no one quite yet knew it at the time. One week earlier at Sun Records in Memphis, a skinny kid named Elvis Presley had cut his first commercial record, "That's All Right," a slightly up-tempo version of a 1946 blues song originally titled, "That's All Right Mama." The song came in at less than 2 minutes and Elvis would go on to revolutionize the music business and become an American icon with nearly a billion records sold by the end of the century.

Atop the best seller list in literature, *Not as a Stranger* by Morton Thompson topped the fiction side of things while *The Power of Positive*

Thinking by Norman Vincent Peale was dominating the nonfiction side of the ledger. Thompson's novel followed the life of a doctor and his trials and eventual personal growth. Although it was made into a movie the following year, it fell quickly into obscurity.

Peale's work was in the middle of a run that would see it on the best seller lists for more than three years. His self-help book sold millions of copies and was read by millions more, and is still being read today. He was not without his critics. In particular, he was panned for attributing statements and positions to prominent physicians and mental health experts without always naming them.

In cinema, 1954 was a good year and at the time of the All Star break the leading box office draw was *The Caine Mutiny*. Humphrey Bogart starred in the World War II tale of a mentally unstable Navy captain whose crew rebels and seizes his ship and of the courtroom drama that follows. Due out later in the month was *On the Waterfront*, a gritty story of union longshoremen corruption and violence, starring Marlon Brando, which went on to win eight Oscars including Best Picture and Brando as Best Actor. Another classic due out just after that was the thriller, *Rear Window*, starring Jimmy Stewart.

The movie that had Cleveland abuzz was *Magnificent Obsession,* produced by Clevelander Ross Hunter, which would make its world premiere in Cleveland on July 15. Coming to town for the glitzy debut at the RKO Palace Theater were stars Agnes Moorhead and Jane Wyman, the former wife of future President Ronald Reagan. The movie, which also starred Rock Hudson, carried the tagline, "The story of a woman's need for man that will become one of the great emotional thrills of your lifetime." Jane Wyman was Oscar-nominated for Best Actress but did not win. In a week in which the All Star game came to Cleveland, a bit of Hollywood came as well.

Ninth Inning

Coming into the game in the top of the ninth inning for the American League was Chicago White Sox pitcher Virgil "Fire" Trucks playing in his second of two All Star games. Trucks was a minor league fireballer who once struck out 418 batters in a season (the major league record is 383) before joining the Detroit Tigers in 1941. He joined the Navy after the 1943 season, was discharged in late September 1945, and about a week later pitched Detroit to victory in game two of the World Series.

He would have a "remarkable" year in 1952 for the Tigers when he won only 5 games and lost 19—remarkable because two of those five wins were no-hitters—one of only four pitchers ever to have two no-hitters in a single season. He suffered from a lack of run support that year from a brutally bad Tigers team that went 50–104. Also coming into the game for the American League was New York Yankees outfielder Irv Noren, taking over for Ted Williams, and playing in his only All Star game. He was having a career year however, leading the American League in batting average at the break with a .344 mark. He played for six teams from 1950-to-1960, picking up World Series rings with the Yankees in 1952 and 1953, and several more as a coach with the Oakland A's from 1972-to-1974.

In the top of the ninth inning with Trucks on the mound for the American League, Duke Snider drew a walk bringing the tying run to the plate with nobody out. Baseball's perfect warrior and knight, Stan Musial stepped to the plate as apprehension rippled through the stands.

Musial brought the fans to their feet as he shot a line drive down the right field line that hooked into the seats: foul ball. They'd barely had a chance to get back in their seats when he ripped another one down the line and again it bent around the wrong side of the foul pole. Musial then smashed one off the chest of the first baseman, who recovered and stepped on the bag for the out. Gil Hodges popped out to second base which left it up to Handsome Ransome Jackson—who popped one straight up in the air.

Yogi Berra tossed away his catcher's mask and backed into the shadows behind home plate as the fans rose to their feet. He squinted into the hot blue sky above the high roof of Municipal Stadium and at 4:43 P.M. squeezed the ball into his mitt as the highest-scoring All Star game in history came to an end. Final score: American League 11, National League 9.

Happy fans stood cheering and clapping as the American League had won its first All Star game since 1949. The players shook hands and slowly filed off the field, many destined to join the ranks of baseball's immortals and legends one day. The stadium ramps filled as thousands trudged back down toward street level, buzzing about the afternoon that had been. It was the golden age of baseball, and the game reflected that with power, production, vitality, and confidence—much a mirror of the country at the time.

The big arena became quiet and empty as hundreds of sportswriters in the press box pounded their typewriters to file their stories by deadline. Cooling shadows grew longer across the land and at 8:37 P.M., the sun made a fiery plunge over the Lake Erie horizon. It had been a good day in Cleveland, Ohio, a very good day. It had been a good day in America too.

EPILOGUE

It had been a summer of baseball dreams for the city of Cleveland with the thrilling All Star game and the juggernaut Indians steamrolling their way to a major league record 111 wins, ending the Yankees 5-year reign as American League champs. The Indians flew to New York to take on the Giants in the World Series, and victory seemed but a mere formality for the heavily favored Tribe. But things changed on a sunny afternoon on September 29, 1954, a day that a *Plain Dealer* headline predicted, "Indians Will Win in Six." For that was the day the Giants' Willie Mays made what has become known to baseball simply as, "The Catch."

The World Series game one grab that defied reality, a catch so impossible that the NBC-TV announcer referred to it as an "optical illusion," was so much more than an outfield play. It was one of those life-changing events where gnawing doubt devours confidence, where fear of failure parches the throat and tightens the chest, and where the possible becomes impossible.

Not too long after that, the Indians, and the city of Cleveland itself, began to unravel and to sum up—it's all Mays's fault. For years, Clevelanders couldn't believe Mays chased the Vic Wertz blast 460 feet into the remote, Polo Grounds canyon of a center field. (Recent, rational, and sober analysis of film of the catch suggests that the ball actually traveled closer to 430 feet. But when it comes to the catch, Clevelanders don't want to be rational—or sober.)

The record shows that after the catch, the Indians were swept in a World Series they were supposed to win, the team gradually went into decades of decline and the city of Cleveland went along for the ride. Factories and businesses closed and population moved away. The Cuyahoga River caught on fire in 1969, a day that lives in Cleveland infamy, and 3 years later, so did the mayor's hair. And that same mayor's wife declined a White House invitation from First Lady Pat Nixon because it was her bowling night.

With an eroded tax base and municipal debt piled up—in 1978, Cleveland became the first American city since the Great Depression to go into default, and the Cleveland jokes rolled. Clevelanders observed these events, shook their heads, and said, "That catch. That darn catch. How does a guy get to a ball 480 feet from home plate anyway!"

The worst of it was that there was no real villain to the story for, if anything, Willie Mays was the antivillain. "He lit up the room when he came in," said his one-time manager, razor-tongued, Leo "The Lip" Durocher. "He was a joy to be around." And this was the same Leo Durocher who once said, "Nice guys finish last."

Not only did Mays rob Cleveland of a game, a World Series, and the city's self-confidence, he robbed Cleveland fans of righteous indignation, of nursing a grudge, and of that all-important, soothing hatred sports fans everywhere need to indulge in to feel better when things go wrong. Cleveland had been robbed by a nice guy.

But spurred by an urgency that perhaps only a flaming river and mayor can provide, the city came bounding back. New office towers broke the sky at Public Square, their clean, modern lines joining the columned, classical spire of Terminal Tower. Entertainment and shopping districts sprouted and new downtown stadiums and arenas were built. And the dramatic, pyramidal glass and steel edifice of the Rock and Roll Hall of Fame rose in 1995 over a modern harbor from what was once a lakeside, Municipal Stadium parking lot.

That same year, the Indians won their first pennant since the 1954 heartbreak year and Cleveland was called "The Comeback City." The center the *New York Times* once said was worth shouting about was so again; a city a unique synthesis of the grandeur of its past and emerging, modern present. Clevelanders observed these events, nodded their heads in approval and said, "This is great, but you know that Willie Mays was some 500 feet from home plate when he made that catch."

Another pennant followed in 1997 and Cleveland was finally poised to exorcise its baseball demon and christen its new downtown with a World Series parade. That year the Indians, in their 96th year of existence, took on the Florida Marlins, a mercenary-laden, recent expansion team so new that many of its fans weren't sure what a balk or a squeeze play were. The series was tied at three game apiece and redemption lay three outs away in game seven with Cleveland leading 2–1 in the bottom of the ninth inning, despite having a runner thrown out at the plate in the top of the ninth.

On the mound was their veteran closer who'd saved more than 100 games the previous 3 years and who was born in another country—years after the catch. But he couldn't save this one as the Marlins scratched out a run to tie the score and the Indians went on to lose the game, and the World Series, in 11 innings. Salvation had slipped through their fingers like a rope of sand and the closer was bitterly blamed by many Cleveland fans, but it wasn't really his doing. It was Willie Mays, 43 years earlier, streaking 520 feet from home plate that cast the die.

The Indians have lost a bit of momentum since then and the reality remains that no World Series victory parade has wound through the streets of Cleveland since 1948. More than six decades have come and gone. Older generations have traveled their journey and passed on while new ones have grown to adulthood, endowed their children with their Cleveland baseball heritage and moved into middle age.

For Cleveland fans all there is, is time, and all there is to do is savor the smaller victories as they happen and wait. And if necessary, wait some more.

As long as it takes.

Thoughts on Baseball

French novelist and critic Alphonse Karr once said, "plus ça change, plus c'est la même chose" which has been translated to, "the more things change, the more they stay the same." Baseball is a case study in this. Since the 1954 All Star game, baseball has survived dubious changes and events such as steroids, strikes, free agency, bloated salaries, artificial turf, and World Series games lasting past midnight. It has even survived $2,500 single seats in Yankee Stadium, the short pants and floppy-collared uniforms worn by the Chicago White Sox in 1976 and critics who say it's too slow and too boring—which it can be at times.

But in an ever-changing world, baseball still defiantly, and unapologetically, holds on to its basic roots. The game is still played on a 90-foot square infield—just as it was well more than a hundred years ago. The outfield walls are unique in distance from ballpark to ballpark as they've always been. Players still drop their heads and take a measured, even dignified trot around the bases after hitting a home run with no self-celebration. Innings end when the third out is made and each game determines its own time as no clock ticks and no whistle is blown. Every season renews in the freshness of spring, segues into golden days of summer, and comes to an end during the splendor of autumn. The field then sleeps under a blanket of snow waiting for the cycle to begin again.

Baseball stadiums remain a place of revelation for young children who on their very first visit, bound up the walkway to the level of the field and stop dead in their tracks. There the sheer enormity of structure, its green grass expanse and vast ceiling of brilliant blue sky, literally explode before their eyes as their mouths drop open and they stand there amazed.

Such a moment happened to the author in old Municipal Stadium about 1959—as fresh in my memory as if it happened yesterday. There began my lifelong affinity for baseball, the Cleveland Indians and Cleveland itself. The 1960s for me are a reminiscent collage of halcyon, summer day trips to downtown and the giant stadium with my father and childhood friends, of hot dogs and popcorn, and of cheering ourselves hoarse for our Indians and hating the Yankees—as was our civic obligation. My father, who much preferred football to baseball, patiently took me to Indians games anyway.

When boredom came to little boys as it always does, we'd climb to the top row of the vast upper deck. There Lake Erie stretched beyond the horizon. The ships and sailboats on the water looked like toys and we were quite sure we could see Canada. Then to the floor of the lower deck to sneak into field level box seats and see our heroes up close, only to be kicked out by an usher within a few minutes. How did they always know we didn't have tickets for those seats?

At home I would carry around a transistor radio listening to games or go to bed on warm summer nights, with it tucked under my pillow, the hum of the play-by-play crackled by the lightning static of a distant thunderstorm. And in the morning, the rush to check the *Plain Dealer* to find the score, when sleep came before the game ended. Yes, the Indians lost more than they won. No matter.

Beyond baseball, the journeys downtown were special by themselves. For the child's eyes also see the city's stately buildings, the Public Square, the great lake, and the great bridges both from above and below as a freighter carefully squeezes down the Cuyahoga River. And he realizes that this is where he is from, that this is his story.

By the end of the decade my family moved away from Cleveland and visits to my hometown and the old ballpark became less frequent.

The years move on, the stadiums of our childhood are torn down, and our beloved fathers too, get old and die although the bonds remain. No, the Indians have not brought home a World Series title in my lifetime and who knows if they will. But the gifts of heritage and the sense of place are things treasured.

The Rock

In neighborhood sandlot games, arguments often played out over who would get to "be" their favorite Cleveland player but it was always over the same one—Rocky Colavito. A slugging right fielder with a cannon for an arm, he could throw a ball from home plate over the center-field fence. In 1959 he blasted four consecutive home runs in a game, the only Indian to ever do it, and went on that year to bring home the American League home run title. And few players signed as many autographs as he did. Tall, handsome, popular and just plain supercool, everyone wanted to be Rocky.

To be Rocky was to imitate his batting ritual. He'd first hold the bat behind his neck and stretch from side to side, pull his cap low over his eyes then step into the batters box. He'd take a couple of practice swings and pause and point the bat directly, and menacingly, at the mound, then slowly cock the bat just above his right shoulder and lock his dark Italian eyes on the pitcher. And if you didn't do the imitation just right, your peers would let you know.

But the unthinkable happened at the beginning of the 1960 season when Cleveland's restless general manager (GM), who traded players the way kids traded baseball cards, shipped him to Detroit for an aging singles hitter. It was an act of sheer betrayal, if not lunacy—stadium protestors carried an effigy of the GM in a coffin but to no avail— "The Rock" was gone. (The trade is merely considered to be The Worst in team history and, by many, a catalyst for the decades of futility that followed).

Though in exile to a faraway city where he was never as popular, we still argued over who got to be Rocky on summery, little league days. Then in 1965 the wrong was righted and he returned, though it cost the Indians a bundle in a trade. And even past his prime, he stepped right back into his demigod shoes and led the league in RBI's, made the All Star team, and played 162 errorless games, his howitzer arm making baserunners think twice about advancing on any ball hit his way. Rocky was back in right field like he had never left and things made sense again. The team didn't win a whole lot more but "Don't knock the Rock," was the word in Cleveland and no one ever did. And they still don't.

In the deep recesses of center field in Progressive Field where the Indians now play stands Heritage Park, monuments in stone and bronze to the best players in team history. On one stands the frozen image of Rocky, bat cocked just above his right shoulder, eyes fixed toward the mound. If time could be reversed and he could stand at home plate again, kids across the Cleveland area would once more argue whose turn it was to be Rocky on dusty, Cleveland area ball fields on sultry, summer days.

Plus ça change, plus c'est la même chose. The more things change, the more the stay the same.

APPENDIX

Acknowledgments

The author would like to acknowledge the following for permission for use of material.

The Baltimore Sun
The Billings Gazette
The (Cleveland) *Plain Dealer*
The Detroit Free Press
Emmetsburg (Iowa) *Reporter/Democrat*
The Los Angeles Times
The (Toledo) *Blade*
New Directions Publishing Corp.

All Star Game Records Broken in 1954

Most Hits by Both Teams—31 (American 17, National 14)
Most Hits by One Team—17 (American)
Most Runs by Both Teams—20 (American 11, National 9)
Most Pitchers Used by Both Teams—13 (American 7, National 6)
Most Pitchers Used by One Team—7 (American)
Gross Receipts—$292,678

All Star Game Records Tied in 1954

Most Home Runs by One Player—2 (Al Rosen, Cleveland)

Most RBI by One Player—5 (Al Rosen, Cleveland)

Most Home Runs by Both Teams—6 (American 4, National 2)

Most Home Runs by One Team—4 (American)

SELECTED BIBLIOGRAPHY

Barra, Allen. *Yogi Berra: Eternal Yankee*. New York: W.W. Norton & Co., 2009.

Bowen, Ezra (ed.) et al. *Shadow of the Atom, 1950–1960*. Alexandria, VA: Time-Life Books, 1970.

Campanella, Roy. *It's Good to be Alive*. Boston: Little, Brown and Co., 1959.

Castro, Tony. *Mickey Mantle: America's Prodigal Son*. Washington, D.C.: Brassey's Inc., 2002.

Coffey, Frank and Layden, Joseph. *America on Wheels*. Los Angeles: General Publishing Group, 1996.

Connors, Richard J. *A Cycle of Power: The Career of Jersey City Mayor Frank Hague*. Metuchen, NJ: The Scarecrow Press, 1971.

Cormack, George (ed.). *Municipal Stadium: Memories on the Lakefront*. Cleveland: Instant Concepts. 1997.

Creamer, Robert W. *Stengel: His Life and Times*. New York: Simon and Schuster, 1984.

Douglas, George H. *The Golden Age of the Newspaper*. Westport, CT: Greenwood Press, 1999.

Eisenhower, Dwight. D., et al. *The Diaries of Dwight D. Eisenhower, 1953–1961: Microfilmed from the holdings of the Dwight D. Eisenhower Library*. Frederick, MD: University Publications of America., 1987.

Eskenazi, Gerald. *Bill Veeck: A Baseball Legend*. New York: McGraw-Hill, 1988.

Ewald, Dan. *John Fetzer: On a Handshake*. Champaign, IL: Sagamore Publishing, 1997.

Flint, Jerry. *The Dream Machine: The Golden Age of American Automobiles*. The New York Times Book Co., 1976.

Garza, Hedda. *Frida Kahlo*. New York: Chelsea House Publishers, 1994.

Glazier, Willard (Capt.). *Peculiarities of American Cities*. Philadelphia: Hubbard Brother, 1884.

Halberstam, David. *The Fifties*. New York: Villard Books, 1993.

Harper, William A. *How You Played the Game: The Life of Grantland Rice*. Columbia: The University of Missouri Press, 1999.

Jackson, John A. *Big Beat Heat: Alan Freed and the Early Years of Rock & Roll*. New York: Macmillian Publishing Co., 1991.

Kahn, Roger. *The Boys of Summer*. New York: Harper & Row, 1972.

Flory, "Kelly" J. *American Cars, 1946 to 1959*. Jefferson NC: McFarland & Co. Inc., 2008.

Kearns, Doris. *Lyndon Johnson and the American Dream*. New York: Harper & Row, 1976.

Kelly, Barbara. *Expanding the American Dream: Building and Rebuilding Levittown*. Albany: State University of New York Press, 1993.

Kiepper, James J. *Styles Bridges: Yankee Senator*. Sugar Hill, NH: Phoenix Publishing, 2001.

Kluger, Richard. *The Paper: The Life and Death of the New York Herald Tribune*. New York: Alfred A. Knopf, 1986.

Layman, David (ed.) *American Decades: 1950–1959*. Detroit: Gale Research Inc., 1994.

Lindbergh, Charles A. *Autobiography of Values*. New York: Harcourt Brace Jovanovich, 1976.

McKean, Dayton David. *The Boss: The Hague Machine in Action*. New York: Russell & Russell, 1940.

Miller, Carol Poh and Wheeler, Robert. *Cleveland: A Concise History. 1796–1990*. Bloomington: Indiana University Press, 1990.

Moffi, Larry and Kronstadt, Johnathon. *Crossing the Line: Black Major Leaguers, 1947–1959*. Iowa City: University of Iowa Press, 1994.

Montville, Leigh. *Ted Williams: Biography of an American Hero*. New York: Doubleday, 2004.

Moore, Joseph Thomas. *Pride Against Prejudice: The Biography of Larry Doby*. New York: Greenwood Press, 1988.

Neff, James. *The Wrong Man*. New York: Random House, 2001.

Nemec, David, et al. *Players of Cooperstown*. Lincolnwood, IL: Publications International, Ltd., 1993.

O'Neal, Bill. *The Pacific Coast League, 1903–1988*. Austin, TX: Eakin Press, 1990.

Piersall, Jim and Hirshberg, Al. *Fear Strikes Out*. Boston: Little, Brown, 1955.

Pluto, Terry. *The Curse of Rocky Colavito*. New York: Simon & Schuster, 1994.

Rhodes, Richard. *Dark Sun: The Making of the Hydrogen Bomb*. New York: Touchstone, 1995.

Rose, Reginald. *The Death and Life of Larry Benson*. Chicago: The Dramatic Publishing Co., 1960.

Rosendorf, Neal. "John Foster Dulles' Nuclear Schizophrenia," in John Lewis Gaddis et al., *Cold War Statesmen Confront the Bomb: Nuclear Diplomacy Since 1945*. New York: Oxford Univ. Press, 1999.

Rust, Art Jr. *"Get That Nigger Off the Field."* New York: Delacorte Press, 1976.

Seavey, Nina Gilden, Smith, Jane S. and Wagner, Paul. *A Paralyzing Fear: The Triumph Over Polio In America.* New York: TV Books, LLC., 1998.

Stout, Glenn & Johnson, Dick. *Jackie Robinson: Between the Baselines.* San Francisco: Woodford Press, 1997.

Tibol, Raquel. *Frida Kahlo: An Open Life.* Albuquerque: University of New Mexico Press, 1993.

Torilatt, Lee. "DeVere Baker's Raft Adventures." *Sonoma* (CA) *Historian*, #4, 2006.

Vincent, David, Spatz, Lyle and Smith, David W. *The Midsummer Classic.* Lincoln: University of Nebraska Press, 2001.

Whitfield, Steven J. *The Culture of the Cold War.* Baltimore: The Johns Hopkins University Press, 1991.

Wright, Marshall D. *The Southern Association in Baseball, 1885–1961.* Jefferson, NC: McFarland & Co., 2002.